CHRISTIAN

BODY

POLITIC

CHRISTIAN BODY POLITIC

**21st Century Reformed Christian
Perspectives on Church and State**

Edited by

Christian Kim

The Hermit Kingdom Press
Cheltenham ♦ Seoul ♦ Bangalore ♦ Cebu

CHRISTIAN BODY POLITIC
21st Century Reformed Christian
Perspectives on Church and State

ISBN 0-972-38644-0

For information address:

The Hermit Kingdom Press
Suite 407
3741 Walnut Street
Philadelphia, PA 19104
USA

www.TheHermitKingdomPress.com

Dedicated to all,
regardless of race, ethnicity, color, background,
who have taken up the cross
in loyalty to Jesus Christ and His Church

Contents

Preface

Discussions regarding the relationship between church and state seem to predominate political discussions, religious discourse, personal conversations, court cases, and academic publications. This volume is an effort to add some food for thought in the midst of all this. All the contributors are professing Christians who have been profoundly influenced by the Reformed faith, a Christian tradition going all the way back to St. Augustine and beyond. All of us would like to be of help to all Christians, regardless of denomination. We hope that the articles contained in this volume will help you answer some of your questions regarding the relationship between church and state and spur you to further study of Biblical principles.

Christian Kim
Jesus College
Cambridge
Good Friday 2004

"Die Kirche hat das Recht, für sich und die Erfüllung ihres Auftrags den Schutz des Staates in Anspruch zu nehmen, sofern sie dadurch weder dem Staat ein Mitspracherecht über die Wahrnehmung ihres Auftrags einräumt noch sich seiner Sanktionsmöglichkeiten für die Verwirklichung ihres kirchlichen Auftrags bedient."

Wilfried Härle

Dogmatik

"There Is Another King": Gospel as Politics Notes Towards a Theology of Community

Stephen Joel Garver

La Salle University
Philadelphia, USA

Introduction

When Paul and Silas were accused by a mob in Thessalonika, among the charges brought against them was that they proclaimed that there is another king, this Jesus (Acts 17:7). Whatever the intentions of the mob may have been, this incident shows us that the Gospel message heralded by Paul -- that Jesus, as the messiah, has been made Lord -- was a message easily and credibly heard as a political message in the context of the ancient world.[1] This was even so when those bearing that message were busy with what we

---

[1] N. T. Wright likewise suggests that the message Paul brings here is politically resonant (2000:165).

would see as "church work": proclaiming Jesus, explaining the Scriptures, and baptizing converts.

And yet, in our world, the Gospel is often heard only as a message about personal salvation or about distant events in a distant history or the promise of a new kind of spiritual experience. Even where the Gospel does lead to political involvement, more often than not it is seen as the intrusion of religion or the church into secular space, either by projecting one's private religiosity into the public square or by dangerously colluding with the powers that be or by attempting to wrest their power from them.[2]

In the following essay, I will argue that the way things now stand is deficient and that the Gospel does not merely lead Christians to enter into and engage themselves within secular political space. Rather the Gospel *is* politics, a politics moreover that questions the very constitution of any social space as "secular" or the relegation of politics to that space.[3]

The Gospel, thereby, begins to redefine what we mean by "politics," allowing our understanding of the political to migrate from ordinary understandings of it in narrow terms of civil administration (whether presupposing "secular" space or not), to a broader, analogically refracted concept of politics as encompassing the entire ethics of community and its common good, preserving politics as a normative discourse and practice embracing the various structures and patterns of human association under authority.[4]

---

[2] It seems to me that many well-intentioned Christians are, unfortunately, complicit in these misunderstandings (much of the rhetoric of the so-called Religious Right comes to mind, though left-leaning bodies such as the National Council of Churches are often just as imprudent). Part of the burden of this essay is an attempt to rethink these problematics.

[3] This is not to say, by any means, that politics is the *primary* focus of the Gospel and, much less, that politics somehow *exhausts* the meaning of the Gospel. But inasmuch as the relationship between faith and politics is the aim of this essay, I will be focusing upon the political import of the Gospel.

[4] I am appealing here, in part, to the pre-modern notion of the "political" as a very broad ethical discourse, encompassing various forms of human association, the virtues embodied in them, directed toward the common good as an end, and exercised through some kind of public authority (though, unlike ancient political

Moreover, though our everyday grasp of the political may *begin* in our encounter with the sphere of civil magistracy, my claim is that, ontologically speaking, politics is rightly founded in the claims of the Gospel and the establishment of the church.[5]

I will begin by examining and deconstructing the notion of the "secular" as an artifact of the Enlightenment, noting how it has come to constrain the ways in which Christians and the church have seen themselves as related to the political. In the second half of this essay, I will attempt to sketch the ways in which the Gospel refashions politics around itself through its very message about a new King and new Lord, through the establishment of the church as the center of God's reign, and through new practices -- in particular, baptism and eucharist -- which are themselves politically transformative.

Deconstructing the "Secular"

In order for the politics of the Gospel to be heard and grasped, it is first necessary to dismantle some of the assumptions that are often brought to discussions of civil order and faith, assumptions that may well distort what is meant by the claim that the Gospel is politics. These assumptions are typically "modern" -- the "modern" referring to those varying perspectives that have been widely operative since the 17th century and which share many common themes and notions, ranging over the realms of politics, epistemology, ethics, and metaphysics.[6]

---

thinkers such as Aristotle, I would place politics under the wider rubric of ethics, rather than vice versa). As such, the church can be seen as "political" in a way analogous to a particular civil regime or, perhaps, "counter-political."

[5] One thinks here of Augustine's claim that the Roman empire could not claim truly to be a republic or a people since it lacked justice, other virtues, and authentic community (*De Civitatis Dei* 19.21-28). Augustine goes onto suggest that it is the church that is the true *res publica* and city-state.

[6] Much of the following analysis is drawn from de Certeau 1992, Foucault 1994, Gillespie 1994, Milbank 1993, Montag 1999, and Pickstock 1998. The story of

Such assumptions include: the conception of the "secular" as a particular social space as opposed to the religious; a limiting of the "political" to that secular space and conceiving it primarily in terms of struggle for power; an abstract opposition between "society" and the "individual" or the public and the private.[7] These assumptions, in turn, are tied up with more evidently theological ones: a separation of reason and faith; a sharp division between the order of nature and that of grace or the natural and supernatural; a dichotomization between the exterior or objective and the interior or subjective; and so on. Moreover, it is arguable that this entire set of assumptions involves relations of mutual support and thus comes together as a single "package." I will explicate some of these assumptions and dynamics presently, while leaving the rest to be addressed in my more positive account.

We can begin by noting that the "modern," as many have contended, has its roots not merely in certain philosophical thinkers of the Enlightenment, but (perhaps more importantly) earlier in the late scholastics (e.g., John Duns Scotus, William of Ockham).[8] Thereby, the "modern" also affects in differing degrees the thought of both various varieties of Protestantism as well as Tridentine Catholicism, including the ways in which both developed their

---

the transition from the pre-modern to the modern is one that is gaining an important place within much postmodern discourse as a genealogical strategy by which modernist assumptions can be recovered and questioned.

[7] John Milbank begins his magisterial *Theology and Social Theory* with the assertion, "Once, there was no 'secular'..." (1993:9) and proceeds to narrate the founding of the secular. Much of my account here is dependent upon his.

[8] Although Rene Descartes (1596-1650) is often credited as the "father of modern philosophy," the full story of the construction of the modern is naturally much more complex. After all, Descartes' near contemporaries were also instrumental -- including Niccolo Machiavelli (1469-1527), Petrus Ramus (1515-1572), Jean Bodin (1530-1596), Thomas Hobbes (1588-1679), among others. Consult, e.g., Pickstock 1998:47-100, Milbank 1993:9-38, Gillespie 1994. Moreover, the historical roots of the modern run much deeper, not only philosophically, in the thought of Scotus (1266-1308) and Ockham (1288-1349), but also socially and politically, in developments stemming from the investiture controversy and the rise of conciliarism. On these latter points, consult Montag 1999, Cavanaugh 1998:207-221, de Certeau 1992:82-87, and Kantorowicz 1957.

overall theologies, including their theological reflections upon the state and politics in relation to the church and faith. The full story of the construction of the "modern," with its varying assumptions, however, is beyond the scope of this present essay, but a few brief gestures toward a more complete genealogy may prove useful in questioning its suppositions and categories.

For pre-modern, medieval thought (which finds its highest expressions in Thomas Aquinas and Bonaventure), the kinds of sharp distinctions drawn within the modern were unknown or drawn quite differently. Fundamental to this medieval conception of the world was a conception of language and thought (and, indeed, reality itself) as functioning analogically, grounded upon the doctrine of creation.[9] Since the creation comes from God, is directed towards God, and stands in relation to God, it is like God and revelatory of God. Nevertheless, this revelatory likeness is only analogous -- implying both likeness and unlikeness. Since everything is created by *God* it images him (supremely human beings); but since everything is *created* by God it images him only within the greater and absolute divide between Creator and creature. The Fourth Lateran Council had formulated this in the following way: for every similarity between God and the creature there is an even greater dissimilarity (*maior dissimilitudo in tanta similitudine*).[10]

Thus, for example, when we say "God exists" and "creatures exist" we are using the term "exists" analogously, not univocally (and not equivocally either, since a real likeness is there). For God to "exist" is for him to exist non-derivatively, independently, originally, *a se*, and so on. For us to "exist" is to exist derivatively,

---

[9] One may speak here of an *analogia entis*, though the term came into current use through Erich Przywara in the early 20th century. The criticism of this notion by Karl Barth and some other (Reformed) Protestant authors, seems to me to largely miss the mark by understanding the *analogia* in far too a post-scotistic manner.

[10] For a very helpful exposition of this doctrine of analogy and its implications for faith, philosophy, politics, education, gender, and the like, see Schindler 1996. Schindler follows very closely in the footsteps of de Lubac and von Balthasar on these matters.

dependently, createdly, *in deus*, and so on. In God, existence and essence are co-terminous and identical. In the creature, there is a real distinction between existence and essence (i.e., we don't *have* to exist) that gives primacy to act over form as the concrete and particular subsistence of things. Nevertheless, because of creation, there are real analogies between the divine existence and creaturely existence.

This analogical view has implications for many areas of thought and practice, including not only epistemology and metaphysics, but also (and more importantly for our present purposes) political theology and philosophy. But I begin with a metaphysical observation, that within this pre-modern perspective the "natural" is not the self-contained world of manipulable matter that is the opposite of "artificial" (as it became in later thought) and thus the "supernatural" is not conceived as some second story of "stuff" that is somehow added on top of a more basic nature. On the contrary, *natural* has to do with kinds of things, their origins and ends, and what they do (including making "artificial" things), as they are organized in relation to one another in a single whole. All things within their fundamental relations to other things within this whole are "natural." Those very *same* things, however, are equally conceived as "supernatural" in terms of their absolute origins (since all creation is ultimately pure gift, i.e., grace) and in terms of their final end (since life within God is the graciously given goal of all creation). "Natural" and "supernatural," therefore, are adjectival or adverbial on such a conception and have no reference to a distinction in substance. They are also temporal, pointing backward and forward in the unfolding of time, rather than spatial. Nature, indeed, is always-already "graced." [11]

---

[11] While a sharp dichotomy between "nature" and "grace" or the "natural" and the "supernatural" is often taken to be a hallmark of the thought of Thomas Aquinas, this is a serious confusion, mistaking the views of later thomism (which is much indebted to Cajetan and Suarez) for those of the Angelic Doctor himself. Much of the burden of 20th century Roman Catholic theology has been to move beyond these dichotomies towards a more integrated -- and more authentically thomist -- understanding of nature and grace. The two most important figures here are Karl

Let us turn now to another observation, this time epistemological. Given what we have already seen about the term "exists" and the relationship between nature and the supernatural, it is clear that on such a pre-modern doctrine of analogy, the question of "Being" cannot be raised apart from the question of created or uncreated being and so there is no possibility of a philosophical ontology that is prior to and unconstrained by theology. Indeed, all of created being must be seen as symbolically disclosing the divine, pointing to transcendent reality, not just as some undifferentiated "God of the Philosophers" but as the Triune God of Scripture. This is the case, in part, because all of the perfections of God (truth, being, goodness, beauty, etc.) are only manifest in the generation of the Logos in the Spirit. Thus our knowledge of God, ourselves, and the world is an analogous manifestation in us of God's own Trinitarian knowledge of these things and thereby, as it were, our thinking God's thoughts after him.[12]

With regard to the political, there are significant implications following from these observations, foremost that it is impossible to construct some kind of "natural" or wholly "common grace" politics that remains neutral to and outside of theological concerns and the operation of grace in history. On the other hand, there can be no simplistic identification between the structures, role, and significance of the various overlapping organizations of, for instance, church and civil orders. Rather, their relationship must be conceived analogically, within the eschatological tension of creation's origin and end. Thus the pre-modern notion of the "*saeculum*" was not that of the modern spatialized "secular." Rather, it was temporal, referring to those aspects of the present order of things that will one day pass away when the *telos* of the creation is consummated.

Rahner (see Rahner 1992; 1978) and Henri de Lubac (see de Lubac 1998; 1984), though the retrieval of Aquinas is a much broader project; see Chenu 1964, Jordan 1992, te Velde 1992, O'Rourke 1992, Jenkins 1997, Milbank and Pickstock 2001, and Kerr 2002.

[12] Milbank and Pickstock's *Truth in Aquinas* (2001) presents an extended exposition and defense of interpreting Aquinas in this way.

This also implies that "politics" is not to be confined to the functioning of power within a secular realm, but must, first of all, refer very broadly to the whole organization of a *"polis,"* a way of life of a people who share a common life, including various analogous and overlapping structures of rule and authority (what one might see as an irreducibly "gothic" social space).[13] These implications will be drawn out further below in relation to the Gospel, church, and sacraments.

Before turning to that account, however, we can note that there were several important shifts that John Duns Scotus (and later, Ockham and nominalism) introduced into wider questions as they had been explicated within pre-modern thought. The major Scotistic shift was the positing of a univocal notion of "Being" and with that, undermining the analogical use of language.

Unlike his medieval predecessors, Scotus maintained that it is possible to consider "Being" in abstraction from the question of created or uncreated being. In doing this Scotus established the separation of philosophy (ontology and epistemology) from theology and, indeed, founded the possibility of constructing a philosophical ontology that is unconstrained by and transcendentally prior to theology itself, philosophy thereby being permitted to set the conditions for theology. Ockham, in turn, represents a further radicalization of the steps that Scotus had already taken, positing an entirely equivocal notion of "Being" in dialectical tension with its univocity.

Other separations and dichotomies (nature/grace, nature/supernature, faith/reason) flow from these basic shifts in the following ways. First, God and creation can be set within one undifferentiated chain of Being. This, however, introduces serious difficulties into language and its ability to refer since "Being" can now refer univocally to two different realities -- created and uncreated -- and thus language, and our ideas and concepts expressed in language, become a mask over reality rather than a

---

[13] On the notion of "complex" or "gothic" social space, see Cavanaugh 2002:99-106 and Milbank 1997:268-292.

medium by which reality is able to reveal itself to us in the context of the event of knowing.

This in turn begins to shift epistemology into a direction in which the subject and object of knowledge become increasingly related extrinsically and externally, rather than maintaining the kind of interior intentional connection that was found in earlier thought. Thus it is the case that either the world exterior to the mind remains philosophically unknowable or it becomes approachable only through experimental manipulations devised by reason, perhaps guaranteed by divine fiat (as was true both for Ockham and, later, Descartes). Thus, late medieval thought unwittingly founded what would develop into the claims of Enlightenment reason.

With regard to nature and supernature (and its concomitant, nature and grace), there is a twofold separation and fission between God and the creation (even if Scotus' original intent was to safeguard the gratuity of grace). First, since God and creation are both situated within a single extension, it is possible to explain and think about the world in relation to Being without reference to God and thus the world becomes the self-enclosed system of "nature," a material reality that remains complete in itself and at our disposal. It is this "nature" that opens up the space for the secular and politics as one expression of the exercise of power over that realm.

Second, this entails that the operation of grace must be seen as an extrinsic operation that is super-added from outside of the creation and thus is, experientially, unknowable except by faith (even if otherwise guaranteed by revealed facts such as "propositional revelation" or by grace-given experiences such as "being born again" or externally imposed present authority such as "papal infallibility" or automated sacramental mechanisms).[14]

---

[14] On the move away from pre-modern notions of *revelatio*, consult the account given by Montag 1999. The rejection of medieval typological and liturgical enactments of the biblical text and the decided shift towards a more literalistic exegesis and the "grammatico-historical" sense of the text, was deeply complicit with the founding of the modern as well as the construction of the secular state. See Milbank's comments on the biblical hermeneutics of Hobbes and Spinoza in 1993:17-20.

Religion, thus, begins to be pushed to the margins of what is distinctively human, a development that will have significant implications for the Renaissance isolation of the "secular" as a particular space of human existence, under the sole scrutiny of human reason.[15]   Such a space exists in distinction from the privatized and interiorized realm of a grace accessible only by faith, a site that was constructed by late medieval theology and philosophy.[16]

By the time the "modern" fully emerged, it arrived with a well-formed secular sphere to which politics is proper, leaving us with the various negotiations between that sphere and "religion" to which I already referred above.   Regularly enough, political theology has been complicit -- often unwittingly -- with these modernist assumptions, even within those traditions that most wish to be consciously "biblicist" in their approach.

In the Reformed tradition, for instance, certain theonomic, pluralist, and klinean approaches are arguably all infected to varying degrees (and often in opposite ways) by the erection of secular social space. In the case of some theonomic thought, the rhetoric and strategy remains very much one of power, taking over present political structures (even if emphasizing bottom-up efforts, limited government, and rule of law) without substantially questioning the nature and constitution of modern social space and its underpinnings (e.g., an abstract opposition between the individual and society, the

---

[15] Indeed, the very notion of "religion" underwent a significant shift, see Cantwell Smith 1962:30-44.

[16] Again, consult the critiques of this perspective by Rahner and de Lubac (though my sympathies lie with de Lubac, in the context of Catholic debates). This conceptualization of "nature" and "grace" was the standard account within Roman Catholic dogmatics texts by the time of the 19th century and remained prominent in Roman Catholic theology well into the 20th century. I would argue that these very same dynamics play out in analogous way, particularly within some Reformed Protestant dogmatics, in areas such as how the doctrine of "regeneration" relates to Christian experience or the relationship between the pre-lapsarian "covenant of works" and the "covenant of grace." Various attempts to overcome the more problematic forms these dynamics have met with considerable resistance in some quarters.

market as a neutral mechanism of exchange).[17] In the case of some pluralisms (however "principled") and of klineanism, there are varying degrees of retreat from theological engagement with the political, staking out a sealed sphere of kingdom work (often centered on personal, individual salvation) and only entering the secular sphere on the basis of a naturalistic "common grace" that remains neutral to Jesus.[18]

Obviously these claims cannot be taken to characterize all versions of the positions in question or to constitute a substantive critique of them. Nonetheless, these kinds of critiques will be borne out, I think, by the more positive account I will provide below. With this genealogical sketch of the modern and its effects in mind, however, we can now turn to the biblical text, hopefully with ears better attuned to hear the politics of the Gospel.

---

[17] I readily admit that the bulk of theonomic literature envisions their program as coming to fruition through evangelism and discipleship. But the question remains: when enough people have converted and have embraced the theonomic vision, what then? I am left with impression that the goal is more for existing institutions to be merely "taken over" by the new majority than for the entire social fabric to be transformed. I say this, in part, because much theonomic analysis of culture and economics remains thoroughly imbued with what strikes me as conventional social conservativism and libertarian economics.

[18] Again, I certainly grant that the intention of these theorists is well-meaning. Several aims may be intended, I presume: [1] to prevent the grace of the Gospel from being confused with mere civil legalities, [2] to realistically recognize that we live in a pluralistic society, and [3] to avoid any kind of "theocracy" (by which is meant, I think, an "ecclesiocracy"). I hope that I am not ignoring any of these concerns, but a couple of comments seem in order. With regard to [1], there are ways of expressing the grace of the Gospel that give in too much on nature/grace dualities; proper distinctions can be made without conceding to such conceptions. With regard to [2], I suggest below that within a Christian politics, a pluralistic society can only be rightly predicated upon the Gospel's call to love even our enemies; such a pluralism cannot remain neutral to the person of Jesus. With regard to [3], the fear of "theocracy" already supposes a distribution of social space in which the church and "religion" is external to the civil sphere and thus must intrude upon it in an ecclesiocratic manner in order to shape the political. It is just such a conceptualization I am arguing against as too complicit with the modern.

Gospel as Politics

We start with the simple observation that Jesus (and John the baptizer before him) came with the Good News of a *kingdom* -- the reign of God -- proclaiming the forgiveness of sins. Paul summarized this same Gospel in terms of the one who "was descended from David according to the flesh and was declared to be the son of God in power according to the Spirit of holiness by his resurrection from the dead: Jesus, the messianic king, our Lord" (Rom 1:3-4), then going on to expound justification. Such a Gospel not only presents itself as the proper fulfillment of the political aspirations of Israel (no matter how much it may challenge, overturn, and redefine those aspirations), but also, insofar as it became Good News for all people, Jew and Gentile alike, it relativized or undercut any claim by Caesar to be ultimate Lord, ruler, savior, or divine son.[19]

In the following sections, then, I will argue that this Gospel (even the very term "Gospel") is fraught with politically disruptive claims and thereby gives rise to a new kind of civil community in the church, which practices two politically redefining rites: baptism and eucharist. Thus, the Gospel is politics and, in its politics, both repositions the relationship between the Christian community and any particular civil governing regime in a way that lies beyond the "secular," as well as shapes and forms how Christians are to act politically.

---

[19] Though perhaps unsatisfactory to some, it is my understanding of the New Testament that the term "Gospel" most focally means the announcement of the reign of God, manifest particularly in the death and resurrection of Jesus as messiah and Lord and is summarized in the Christian confession that "Jesus is Lord." Other matters (such as justification and forgiveness of sins) are immediately entailed by this Gospel, while other matters are further implications of and responses to the Gospel (for instance, personal faith). These matters, however, are not the primary referent of the term "Gospel" itself.

Gospel

We can begin by considering the term "Gospel," which, as is commonly recognized, not only finds its way into the New Testament from the prophetic literature of Israel, but also would have significant resonances within the Roman world to which the New Testament addressed itself.[20]

From the perspective of Isaiah 40 and 52, the "Gospel" was the message of Israel's God returning, enthroned in his holy city on behalf of his people, to redeem them, to judge their enemies, and, in so doing, to set the whole world aright. This vision of Israel's restoration was one that, elsewhere in prophetic literature, was filled out in terms of Israel's anointed king and representative, the messiah, in whom her destiny was set and who would be the agent of Yahweh's justice, establishing true order. In either case, it challenged Israel's ultimate allegiances to any other gods or sovereigns and called her to trust her God and his justice, even in the midst of exile.

From the perspective of the wider world of the New Testament, a "Gospel" was the proclamation and celebration of an emperor or king, whether his birth or his rule, and, in Paul's day, it would have had particular relevance with regard to news of the Caesars. Like Israel's "Gospel," this royal summons was intended to elicit a response of allegiance and fidelity.

When the New Testament presents a *Gospel* about Jesus, then we must see both perspectives in play, giving us a prophetic message that is directly and unavoidably political. The proclamation of Jesus as messianic king, savior, and Lord constituted not only a theological message, but also a political confrontation both with Israel's aspirations and collusions as well as with a wider empire, especially where rulers expected worship and sacrifice as well as taxes.[21] And the "obedience of faith" (Rom 1:5)

---

[20] On the meaning and resonances of the term "Gospel," see Wright 1997:39-62; Horsley 2000:164-165.

[21] On the rising Roman imperial cult, see Price 1984.

which this message engendered represented not only a personal appropriation of some "private" religious truth, but also a very public shift in political allegiances, that "there is another king, this Jesus."

The remarkable content and implications of this New Testament Gospel, however, need to be explored further, so that the precise significance and contours of its politics can be better appreciated.

In focusing the Gospel upon Jesus, the New Testament presents the man of Nazareth as the fulfillment of both Yahweh's return and Israel's messianic expectations, the two prophetic threads intertwined and each deepening the meaning of the other.   Thus, when Paul says in Romans that the "Gospel" proclaims that by Jesus' resurrection the Spirit declared him to be messianic "son of God," this points through and beyond the title of Israel's king and representative (1 Sa 7:14; Ps 2:7; 89:4, 26-27; cf. Ex 4:22), to Jesus' divine sonship as Yahweh in the flesh (see, e.g., Rom 10:13, quoting Joel 3:5).   As such Paul's Gospel subverted not only Israel's understanding of her own God, her political hope, and her messianic expectations, but also the imperial good news of Caesar and his claims to divine sonship. We will examine the Jewish and imperial contexts in turn.

First, let us consider the variegated politics of Second Temple Judaism. The landscape here is likely familiar: while some Jews colluded with the Romans and others retreated into the wilderness, the hopes of many were lodged in political and religious liberation from Roman dominance through the leadership of a revolutionary messiah.[22] Within this matrix of revolutionary hope, rituals and sites such as Torah observance, ancestral traditions, the national homeland, and the Temple itself could serve as powerful symbols of that hope and catalysts for action.[23]

---

[22] For some general overviews of the religious climate of first century Judaism consult Sanders 1992, Saldarini 2001, and Hengel 1989.

[23] Though I cannot agree with all of his various assertions, Borg 1984 makes for stimulating reading on this topic.   For a more balanced account, see Wright 1992:369-442.

It was just such politicized symbols that Jesus drew upon as part of the Good News of God's reign, rejecting, relativizing, and redefining those symbols around himself, thereby calling into question dominant Jewish notions of identity and ambition, proposing a different "way" of being the people of God. In doing this, however, Jesus was proposing another kind of politics, one which the Gospel-writers present as the politics of the true messiah and, therefore, of Israel's God, restoring his people and establishing his justice. Indeed, the "way" that Jesus followed is the very "way of Yahweh," which is, paradoxically, the way of the cross.[24]

This was a reversal of all expectations. Rather than overthrowing the Romans and restoring Israel's power and symbols in the way anticipated, this messiah would "be handed over to the chief priests and the scribes, and they will condemn him to death; then they will hand him over to the Gentiles; they will mock him, and spit upon him, and flog him, and kill him…" (Mk 10:33-34; cf. 8:31; 9:31). In his words to his disciples, Jesus made the politics of this reversal explicit:

> You know that those who are considered rulers over the Gentiles Lord it over them, and their great ones are tyrants over them. But it is not so among you; rather, whoever wishes to become great among you must be your servant, and whoever wishes to be first among you must be slave to all. For even the son of man did not come to be served, but to serve, and to give his life as a ransom for many (Mk 10:42-45).

---

[24] Regarding "the way" that Jesus followed, see Mk 2:23; 3:1; etc., esp. 10:17, 32, 52. That Jesus' "way" was the very way of Yahweh is intimated by John the baptizer at the beginning of the Gospel, Mk 1:2-3; that it was the way of the cross is stated by Jesus himself in Mk 8:34-35; 9:35. The centurion at the foot of cross draws these texts together when, seeing the way Jesus died, he confesses, "Surely this was son of God" (Mk 15:39). For a more detailed study of these themes in Mark, see Garver 2000.

It is precisely in the apparent shame and defeat of the cross that Jesus, in fact, had victory over the principalities and powers, putting them to open shame on the way to reconciling all things to himself (Col 2:13-15).

Jesus, thereby, revealed the way of service -- service unto death -- as the true way of being the messianic king. And, insofar as the messiah was the summation and representative of Israel, Jesus lived out in his own life what Israel had been called to do and be for the world -- called to service among the nations as a light and witness to the God who was the creator of the whole world, a God revealed supremely in Jesus. The way of the messiah and of Israel, then, was not to be the way of ethnic pride or nationalistic fervor, of pharisaic zeal or violent revolution.

Nonetheless, in this reversal of expectations, all Israel's hopes were strangely fulfilled, her restoration found in the new community of believers in Jesus, and, as Israel's messiah, through his death and resurrection, Jesus became Lord and savior of the world, including Rome. Israel, after all, was called by God to bear his purposes for the whole human race in Adam, so that when Israel's true son and king was made Lord, his rule would not be merely that of a Jewish monarch, but moreover, as the true human, embody the eschatological dominion that the race of Adam was always intended by God to receive.[25] Where Eden's guardian, Adam, failed to lay down his life for his bride in the face of a bestial serpent, Jesus was faithful unto death, as a servant, and thus became Lord of all, from Israel to the "farthest corners" of the world.

This trajectory is clear not only in the overall shape of Paul's Gospel of the Jewish messiah who is Lord, but also, for instance, in the unfolding narrative of Luke-Acts, with the ascension of the messiah as divine ruler at its thematic center (functioning against the backdrop of Daniel 7).[26] As the royal proclamation of this messiah goes out to Israel in Acts 1-12, it culminates in the sudden death of Herod, Israel's false king (and local agent of Rome) who arrogates

---

[25] This Adam-Christ dynamic is most evident in Paul's writings (esp. Rom 5 and 1 Cor 15).

[26] For a brief elaboration of this reading of Luke-Acts, see Wright 1998.

to himself royal and divine titles that rightly belong to Jesus. Acts 13-28 narrate this same royal proclamation as it makes its way to Rome, to another throne where there sits another ruler who makes similar royal pretenses to divinity. Thus, Jesus reveals the nature of all truly human rule to be, in the first instance, that of cruciform service -- not of Roman identity or divine aspirations, of imperial power or military violence.

In this context we can reflect upon the Good News of the kingdom as involving the "forgiveness of sin" and Paul's Gospel as directly concerning "justification." These two, closely related categories are the obverse side, as it were, of Jesus' death and resurrection by which he was vindicated as Israel's messiah and Lord of the world.[27]

Since Israel remained in disarray and as exiles in their own land as a result of her sin and apostasy, "forgiveness of sins" was part and parcel of return from that exile, of the vindication and restoration, and advancement of the kingdom that Israel expected and her God had promised. This eschatology, however, was realized in an unexpected way in Jesus as Israel's messiah, through the way of the cross, leading to his own resurrection and enthronement, events by which God declared that sin had been forgiven and that Jesus was in the right before the divine court. Since Israel represented all of adamic humanity, Israel's restoration in the messiah's resurrection, in turn, was also the means by which the human race as a whole might be, in the person of Jesus, restored from its exile from paradise, forgiven and vindicated before the divine court, and advanced to the kind of dominion-through-service for which it was created.

Thus the end of history is already accomplished in the midst of history in the person of Jesus as messiah: the true Israel and the true humanity. Moreover, as Paul emphasizes in Romans, these events reveal the remarkable "righteousness" or "justice of God" (e.g., Rom 1:16-17), God's own faithfulness to his covenant

---

[27] The following remarks draw heavily upon Gaffin 1987, Wright 1992, 1997, and Siefrid 2001, among others.

promises to Israel and the human race, acting as righteous judge, setting the world aright. As such, the doctrine of justification has political implications for both Israel and the wider world.

With regard to Israel, it shows that God's justice -- yearned for by the psalmists and prophets -- is not a vindictive justice that favored Israel at the expense of the Gentile nations or one that condoned Israel's own apostasy. Rather, it shows that Jew and Gentile alike were bound over to sin so that God could shower mercy upon all (Rom 11:32). This would have profound implications for Israel's relationship with the Gentiles, relativizing ethnic, political, and ritual boundaries, particularly as Jew and Gentile were woven together in the church (cf. Eph 2:11-22).

With regard to the wider world, Paul's message of justification -- particularly as addressed to the church at *Rome* -- questions prevailing notions of justice, Rome's divinized pretensions to house the goddess *Iustitia*, and the exercise of that virtue within the empire.[28] The Gospel then calls upon those seeking a true measure of justice to place their ultimate allegiance with Jesus as Lord and savior, rather than the emperor or senate (and Paul's comments on the civil magistracy in Romans 13 must be read in this wider context, designed to preclude misreading his polemic as negating all human civil authority under God).

Thus, once again, the Gospel and the doctrine of justification it entails, reveal a reconfiguration of political values. With these points in hand, we can now turn to how the Gospel takes shape in the people of God as the church.[29]

---

[28] See Georgi 1991 and Wright's comments in Horsley 2000:170-173.

[29] Allow me to anticipate a possible objection at this point: that by so thickly nesting the Gospel within the vocabulary and issues of the era in which it was first articulated, one runs the risk of losing the message of the Gospel for us today (thanks to Jim Rogers for pointing this out and for much other helpful criticism). I would reply by arguing that the Gospel only speaks to situations outside of its immediate first century context *because* it is "so thickly nested" within its first century context. The universal is only found in the particular. And that is not to say that it is necessary to understand all the particularities of the immediate context in order to understand the Gospel for one's own time and place. But I am presupposing an ontology here in which history and cultures are analogically

Church

As resurrected Lord, the justification received by Jesus is, in turn, shared with those who receive the Gospel in faith, thereby becoming the messiah's people and partaking in the forgiveness and vindication he secured and received. Thus the church becomes the locus of a new humanity, where we begin to live out what Jesus has done so that God's justice is manifest (2 Cor 5:21). Therefore, insofar as the church is a forgiven and forgiving community of people sharing an ordered common life together, the church also is the practice of a new politics.

That the church is, in some sense, a "political" community should be evident even from the political, social, and economic terminology that the New Testament applies to the church: assembly, kingdom, city, nation, citizenship, community, people,

---

ordered so that all history that preceded Christ typologically anticipated him in more or less obscure ways ("preceded" here including either absolute temporal preceding or in terms of preceding the Gospel's actual arrival). And all history that comes after Christ, on the other hand, is attributable to the event of Christ and its re-narration of everything through the church. Of course, it is the history of Israel and the church that most centrally and fully participate in Christ either by typological anticipation or as an effect, respectively. But this is only so because everything always already reveals Christ in some manner.

Epistemologically, this means that it isn't *necessary* to do this kind of analysis of the first century context in order for the Gospel to have its import and effects in whatever time and place it arrives, because the context of the first century is already analogically anticipated in that site of arrival in such a way that, once the Gospel is received and enacted sacramentally and liturgically in that new time and place, its original effects will be non-identically reproduced. Nonetheless, this kind of historical analysis serves to deepen that event and, I would argue, enhance the Gospel's effectiveness and relevance to our contexts precisely because the more light that is shed on its original context, the more light we shed on our own context and how to receive the Gospel within it as that good news continuously arrives here and now.

partnership, warfare, and so on.[30] The New Testament is rife with political terminology applied to the church, thereby presenting the church itself as the center of a new kind of human community. But the kind of community the church is supposed to be is not the kind of "political" community the world envisions. It is a community that instead follows the way of the cross, one whose weapons are not the world's weapons, and one in which authority is neither by might nor power, but by the Spirit of God, through one-anothering service and openness to risk.

The New Testament draws out this new ecclesial politics in various stories and images. As one example, in Acts we find the Christian *ekklesia* juxtaposed against that of pagan Ephesus and apostate Jerusalem.[31] In common Greek usage, the *ekklesia* of a *polis* was the ordered assembly of its citizens gathered for official business. But Luke ironically narrates the *ekklesia* of Ephesus as a riot where "some cried one thing, and some another, for the assembly was confused and most of them did not know why they had come together" (Acts 19:32, cf. 19:38, 41). The chaos at Ephesus is paralleled in Acts 21 by similar events in Jerusalem, showing that even the city of Yahweh had devolved to the level of a pagan city-state.

Luke's portrayal is all more ironic in that the Greek *polis* was founded on the aspiration to master chaos, to order society, and to exercise justice, all interwoven with the cult of the patron deity, social class and status, and forms of ritual inclusion and exclusion.[32] Jerusalem finds itself acting the part of a Greek *polis*, accusing Paul of bringing disorder, discarding the law, and defiling ritual boundaries. In both cases, however, Luke shows the purported aims

---

[30] On various aspects of this terminology, see Horsley 1997, 2000. For further reflections on the political, public character of the church, see Leithart 1993 and Clapp 1996:44-57.

[31] The following observations are indebted to Leithart 1997a.

[32] On the nature of the ancient city-state, see Polignac 1995, Zaidman and Schmitt Pantel 1989, Dumezil 1970, Alföldy 1985, and Gordon in Beard and North 1990. Hauerwas and Pinches' interaction with Casey's *Pagan Virtue* is also worthy of note (1997:89-112).

of the respective *ekklesiai* to deconstruct into their opposites in the face of the Christian Gospel: Ephesus falling into disarray, miscarrying justice in the heat of human passions and Jerusalem disregarding the legal requirements of Torah, provoking the intervention of Gentile authority.

Both episodes, thereby, uncover the real workings of merely human politics, as Peter Leithart argues,

> In these two incidents Luke pronounces his (and the Lord's) verdict on the old world's ways of ordering human life, on the cultures of the old creation. When the people come together in *ekklesia*, the true character of their civilization is revealed and unmasked. In the assembly, it becomes clear that the future hopes of the world for peace and justice cannot lie with either of the ancient *ekklesiai*, with either the city-state of the Greeks or the temple city of the Jews.[33]

Adamic humanity, left to itself, can only erect temporary measures towards order, measures that, in the face of the Gospel, are revealed as possessing an underlying and inherent violence.

In between the two accounts, however, Luke tells us what happened when the Christian *ekklesia* of Troas came together at the end of Passover, on the first day of the week, to break bread, representing a liturgical alternative to Ephesus and Jerusalem (Acts 20:6-12). Instead of shouting and chaos, we find the people of God gathered, listening to and dialoguing with Paul, a scene so tranquil that poor Eutychus falls asleep. Leithart comments,

> This is not a place of chaos and confusion but a new life, a new order of human life and society. Its assembly is a passage, a Passover, a *transitus* that moves its participants from death to new life,

---

[33] Leithart 1997a.

signified when (at midnight!) Eutychus goes through
the window to his death but is raised to new life and
is received into the feast.

The breaking of bread together here, in eucharist, is a sacramental
alternative to both the temples of Artemis and of Israel, offering not
merely one way of being a community among other options, but
rather "an alternative *ekklesia*, which formed the heart of an
alternative *polis*, an alternative city, an alternative culture, a new
world."[34]

Elsewhere, in his letter to the (overwhelmingly Gentile)
church at the Roman colony of Philippi, Paul provides a similar
challenge, again centered on the Gospel of Jesus as "savior" and
"lord" who is able to "subdue all things under himself" (3:20-21; cf.
2:9-11, alluding to Isa 45:23 and thereby supposing Jesus' divine
status).[35] Though not all of those whom Paul addresses in Philippi
would have shared the privileges of Roman citizenship, the city as
whole did enjoy many benefits of its colonial status, under the
protection of Roman law and culture, and thus could take pride in
that status, a pride which, in the days of Paul, had begun to take
shape in terms of the cult of the emperors.[36]

It is in this context that Paul warns against placing
"confidence in the flesh" (3:4), and instead, whatever privileges the
Philippians may enjoy, to "count them as loss...as dung" in light of
the reign of Jesus as messiah and Lord and our heavenly citizenship
(3:7-8, 20-21). As Paul had noted earlier, since Jesus was God, he
lived the humility of the true God, not seeking to take advantage of
his divine privilege, but taking the form of a servant, following the
way of the cross (2:6-8; a theme we have already seen unfolded in
the Gospels). Following the pattern of Jesus, Paul works through
the implications for his own Jewish privileges, calling upon the
Philippians to do the same with regard to their Roman citizenship.

---

[34] Leithart 1997a.

[35] The following is informed by the comments of Wright in Horsley 2000:173-181
and Oakes 2001.

[36] On the emperor cult, again see Price 1984.

Paul's argument here, while couched in terms of his own experience with Judaism and cast in the language of Jewish slurs against paganism, is offered as what N. T. Wright suggests is a "coded" analogy (speaking in a way that is "safe" for his readers, 3:1), as a viewpoint from which the Roman, Gentile Philippians are to think about their own allegiances and identity (3:15-20; the analogy between non-Christian Judaism and paganism is one that Paul makes elsewhere as well, cf. Gal 4:1-11; Col 2). The "citizenship" of the Philippian church (1:27; 3:20) lies elsewhere, thereby situating them in Philippi, not as a colony of Rome, testifying to and extending Roman privilege, but as a colony of heaven, testifying to Jesus' Lordship and the way of being human that he lived out (note Paul's allusion to ideal humanity drawn from Psalm 8). This, of course, did not eliminate the Roman identity of Paul's readers, but resituated that identity in the messiah and subsumed it to his service. After all, Paul himself was not beyond pressing his own Jewish, Pharasaic, or Roman identities into the service of the Gospel when the occasion required it (Acts 21:40; 22:3, 25; 23:6).

We find a similar dynamic in Peter's first epistle. Whatever the particular citizenship or ethnicity of his readers, Peter several times refers to them as "exiles" and "sojourners" (1:1, 17; 2:11) in light of their new identity in Jesus, the messiah: "you are a chosen race, a kingdom of priests, a holy nation, God's own people" (2:9).

Leading up to this remark, Peter quotes and alludes to Israel's constitution as a nation (1:14-16; 2:5, 9-10), their deliverance from Egypt (1:18-19), and Israel's promised restoration after exile (1:24-25, quoting Isa 40:6-9), applying each of these to the church as God's new restored humanity, a new race and people, a new kingdom and nation. In this context he also alludes to Jesus' kingship over them as Davidic messiah, the one embodying Israel's restoration (2:6 quoting Isa 28:16), the vindicated one admitted to God's temple after enemy oppression (2:7 quoting Ps 118:22; cf. the allusion to Ps 34:8 in 2:2), and the return of Yahweh himself (2:8 quoting Isa 8:14-15).

Thus, according to Peter, the primary identity of these churches, as a community and a people, did not derive from what part of the empire they happened to reside in (cf. 1:1) or from what people they derived their descent. Rather, as those who had been "ransomed from the futile ways inherited from [their] ancestors" (1:18), they rendered obedience to the Lord Jesus as messiah, as those born into a new human family, with the God of Jesus as their Father (1:14, 17-18, 22-25).

This theology, however, might very well be heard by Peter's audience as liberating them from every human obligation outside of the church and freeing them from all merely human authority, relativizing emperors and governors to the point of undermining their legitimate rule altogether. But Peter anticipates such reasoning, agreeing that Christians are a "free people" -- loosed from old allegiances -- but admonishing them not to use this "freedom as a pretext for evil" (2:16). Peter knows his Gospel, with its message of a new king and kingdom, might well lead the Gentiles to "malign [believers] as evildoers," and so he admonishes the churches to "conduct yourselves honorably...that others may see your honorable deeds and glorify God on the day of visitation" (2:12). As a particular application of this call to honorable conduct, Peter writes that they should "accept the authority of every human institution for the sake of the Lord" Jesus and his rule, whether the emperor or provincial governors, honoring their place as those sent by Jesus as messianic king and Lord to punish wrongdoers and to benefit those who do right (2:13-14).

Thus, for Christians, human authorities are re-positioned as expressions of the authority of God himself and of the messianic Lord he has installed as well as reinterpreting those authorities in relation to a new ecclesial identity. This is a theme also sounded by Paul (Rom 13:1-4), whose comments, like Peter's, must be read in a wider context that questions the pretensions of civil authority in light of Jesus' resurrection as Lord and the justice of God.[37]

---

[37] On Romans 13 see O'Donovan 1996:146-148, Elliott 1994:214-226, Wright in Bartholomew 2000:190-191, and Jewett in Horsley 2000:65-68.

Arguably, both Peter and Paul's injunctions to honor the civil authority as servants of God can be traced back to Jesus' well-known statement, "render to Caesar the things that are Caesar's, and to God the things that are God's" (Mt 22:21), given in answer to a question about paying taxes. In particular, this seems echoed in Paul's statement, "Render to all what is owed to them: taxes to whom taxes are owed, revenue to whom revenue is owed, respect to whom respect is owed, honor to whom honor is owed" (Rom 13:7).

But Jesus' statement, like Peter and Paul's, steers its way through the tension between the ultimate authority of God and sometimes presumptuous human authority, even while affirming that such authority comes from God and pointing out the kind of path that those who would follow Jesus must take.[38] In all three synoptic Gospels the question about paying taxes to Caesar comes in the context of parables of coming judgment upon Jewish unbelief, as well as growing confrontation with Pharisees, Herodians, Sadducees, and scribes. As such, Jesus' reply needs to be read, in part, as a challenge to various Jewish responses to imperial authority, whether revolutionary zeal or expedient compromise, turning the focus instead upon his own identity and mission. Moreover, within the context of the Gospels and the communities to which they were written, Jesus' reply also functions to challenge the church whose identity is found in him.

Jesus begins by asking for a coin and asking whose image and inscription it bore. As any first century person would know, the coin showed Caesar, proclaiming him "son of god" and "high priest," rendering it an extremely problematic object for Jews to carry and use, even not overly scrupulous ones. Jesus' question, then, puts his questioners in an awkward position, face-to-face with what they would resent as their own unsettling complicity in the system they opposed.

Furthermore, the incident occurs in a context where taxation had already spawned more than one revolutionary movement,

---

[38] Some of the following is drawn from Hart 1984, Wright 1992:502-507, and Hays 1996:126-127.

resulting in the execution of the rebels. In this context, Jesus' statement to "Give Caesar what is his" could be heard as an endorsement of such revolutionary programs, a call to stick Rome with its just deserts.[39] But this is the same Jesus who rejected all such programs and called his followers to go the second mile, not to live by the sword, to turn the other cheek, and to be the servants of all. The way of kingdom's victory would be the way of the cross. Thus, Jesus continues, "And give to God what is his."[40] In saying this, Jesus turns the question back to the questioners, challenging where they placed their ultimate loyalties—with their own, potentially violent, political aspirations or with the reign of God that Jesus was proclaiming.

Paul and Peter understand and apply Jesus' teaching rightly. The transformation of political order that Jesus began would come about through being the church as an alternative *polis*, understanding itself as living within an eschatological tension. On one hand, those in the church were called to lead "quiet and peaceable" lives of allegiance to Jesus "in godliness and dignity" (1 Tim 2:2) cooperating with and praying for those in authority in the civil sphere, paying taxes, rendering honor, and serving them as those appointed by God and his messiah.

On the other hand, the church was to enact the reign of God and his triumph in Jesus over the principalities and powers, proclaiming a Gospel message of another king, a citizenship from heaven, and a fearless freedom which resituated all human authority and, when such authority opposed the Gospel itself, could open the path to martyrdom. Indeed, Paul immediately follows his call to "render to all what is owed them" with the paradoxical qualification, "owe no one anything -- except to love one another" (Rom 13:8), thereby resituating even cooperation with political authority in light of the mutual, self-giving love of the Christian community.

---

[39] That Jesus' statement might have been heard this way is all the more possible against the backdrop of a passage like 1 Macc 2:68.

[40] The phrase here resonates with an allusion to Ps 96:7-10, which, given its larger context of Yahweh's contest with false gods and idols, strengthens the anti-imperial undercurrents of Jesus' saying.

Baptism

Baptism is the rite of entrance into this church and kingdom and has, itself, a political dimension, granting a new identity, acting out a new way of forming community, and setting apart those baptized as having already died and risen with the messiah. In all these areas there are important implications for the church as a new *polis* and the practice of a new politics.

In terms of the new identity conferred by Christian baptism, this rite is to be understood in light of Jesus' own baptism and against the background of various water rites in the Old Testament and John the Baptizer's proleptic ministry.[41] As such, baptism is an expression of the faithfulness of *God* himself who, in and through Christ Jesus, accomplished salvation by Jesus' undergoing baptism in his own person for the sake of his people. The baptism of Jesus points back to all of God's acts of creation and re-creation throughout salvation history, including:

- the original creation in which a new world was drawn by God from the watery deep
- the safe journey of Noah and his family through water in God's ship to a new world washed from sin
- the powerful deliverance of Israel from the slavery of Egypt through the cloud and sea unto a new obedience
- the entry of Israel into the promised land, crossing the Jordan, with the ark of God's presence in their midst
- Israel's gracious return from the exile of sin, returning across the great River, vindicating the nation against her enemies.

Jesus' baptism was also a new application of the rites given to God's people for cleansing from the living death of leprosy and from contact with bodily death, rites that had once reconstituted Israelites

---

[41] With regard to what follows, see in particular Garver 1999 and 2001.

as God's priestly people. Analogously, Jesus' baptism recapitulated the ordination of Aaron and his sons as priests to serve in God's house as guardians of his holiness, servants to their Lord, and ministers to his people. Finally, the baptism of Jesus set him apart as heir to David's throne, God's anointed and beloved servant, that is, the representative and sum of Israel's own sonship and her service to the nations as a new adamic people.

Thus, the baptism of Jesus summarized all of God's promises to his people through the centuries -- promises of sonship, priestly service, vindication, spiritual anointing, new creation, God's presence, cleansing, and so on -- and attested to God's faithfulness to all of those promises in the messiah. In Christian baptism, then, everything that belongs to Jesus is shared with his messianic people, the Church, marking them out as God's new creation in which all old barriers have been torn down, whether those of anointed priesthood, ritual purity, familial descent, national identity, or royal lineage. The promises to which these various boundaries once pointed are now fulfilled in the church: the old things have passed away and all is made new.

Thus, within the New Testament, the identity announced in baptism stands in contrast, perhaps most clearly, to the demands of the so-called judaizers. Paul makes it clear, that while such rites had their place in God's plan, no ethnic or nationalistic rite, such as circumcision, marks out the eschatological kingdom. Nor is the rite of kingdom initiation into any kind of gnostic mystery or elaborate induction into citizenship of a pagan *polis*, limited to those who acquired the approved esoteric knowledge, who are born of proper descent, or who have performed some great public work.[42] Rather, baptism stands as a simple, public water rite applicable to all: Jew and Greek, male and female, slave and free, barbarian or Scythian, and so on. All other identities are thoroughly conditioned by baptismal identity and once the kingdom arrives, to return to the old patterns of identity and boundaries, whether Jewish or pagan, would

---

[42] With regard to the religio-political organization of the ancient *polis*, see, again, Polignac 1995, Zaidman and Schmitt Pantel 1989, Dumezil 1970, Alföldy 1985, and Gordon in Beard and North 1990.

be, as Paul says, to submit once again to the "elementary principles" (Gal 4:1-10; Col 2:8-23, where the connection with baptism and "the powers" is made explicit).

Moreover, the new identity received in baptism is one that calls us to die to the old Adam and find our identity in the new Man and the way of life that he established and over which he is Lord. This involves a certain "transvaluation of values," for while there is a lowering and breaching of old adamic barriers, since the church is open to anyone whosoever, there is a cost be counted in such a radical break from old identities, the embracing of a new ecclesial identity, and the forms of social and political tension that may ensue. After all, as Jesus says, those who would follow him must "hate father and mother" if such family ties prove an impediment to following the messianic Lord (Lk 14:26).

Thus baptism is itself an event of considerable social and political risk-taking, marking out a community of such people who, as already dead and reborn, place their ultimate hopes in a kingdom that is not founded upon this world, but proceeds from heaven. Whereas pagan virtue would build political community on the supposition of the community as its own end, ecclesial politics would regard itself as missionary and eschatological in purpose, calling its members, outsiders, and even enemies to that end.[43]

Moreover, the pagan *polis*, as its own end, required that it define itself by a marked distinction between how it treats its own members and how it regards all others. In such a context, the ties that bind people together in community -- both fellow-feeling and anger -- are implicated within a particular kind of communal pride by which co-members share in the nobility of the community itself and those who fail to uphold the standards of the community are deemed worthy of vengeful anger.

Christian practices of the political, however, undermine such conceptions. Paul, after all, regards himself as the apostle to "both to Greeks and to barbarians" (Rom 1:14), setting the two on equal footing with regard to the Gospel's objective. And this

---

[43] On this point and the two that follow, see Hauerwas and Pinches 1997:104-109.

Gospel calls upon all who enter the church to do so through baptism, a recognition that they only come as people who have been forgiven so that any pride in former identities but be regarded as loss. Thus pagan vengeance is undercut and the community puts itself at risk as a place where the onetime enemy is invited within. But, with Jesus as Lord and savior, the Christian church, as a new *polis*, leaves itself to his hands, trusting that he will preserve his people in the world.

Supper

Finally, eucharist is a politically charged meal which projects an ideal for new ecclesial community of forgiven and forgiving people. As such, it has eschatological, environmental, ethical, economic, and other dimensions and thereby must take a central place in any Christian political practice. Given the centrality of the eucharist in any authentic Christian praxis and given its theological depths, my remarks here will be necessarily limited.

In terms of its first century context the eucharist can be read in light of both the sacrificial meals and festivals at the Temple in Jerusalem and over against various kinds of sacred meals within pagan Hellenism. Moreover, our reading of the eucharist must likewise be informed by wider patterns of table fellowship, both in Jesus' own ministry and in the early church.

With regard to Judaism, Jesus' institution of the eucharist in the context of the Passover feast would have certainly drawn upon the significance of that feast, not only as a ritual remembrance of God's deliverance of Israel from Egypt, but also its first century importance as a politicized expression of Israel's hope for present deliverance from Roman occupation and the fulfillment of Yahweh's eschatological promise.[44] Jesus' appropriation of the Passover for his last meal with his disciples must therefore be read, in part, as offering an alternative politics, centered on his own person and the expectation of his imminent execution.

---

[44] On this context for the last supper see Wright 1992:554-563.

In the background to this final meal stood Jesus' practices of table-fellowship which he had undertaken over the three years of his public ministry in which he had "come eating and drinking" as a "friend of tax collectors and sinners" (Mt 11:19). Shared meals, in this cultural environment, embodied close fellowship and, as enacted by Jesus, were both a proclamation of Yahweh's prodigal and restoring forgiveness as well as the construction of new ties of kinship around Jesus himself. As such they called upon participants to extend forgiveness to one another and to all, engendering forms of restitution that exceeded legal requirements. Those at Jesus' table, therefore, were nothing less than the inbreaking of a future eschatological Israel that served as a rebuke against those who would perpetuate a politics of exclusion, national identity, and violence, a rebuke that came to public expression in Jesus' confrontational action at the Temple.[45]

And so, when Jesus gathered his disciples together at Passover (particularly read against Jesus' Temple action earlier that week), he was showing himself and his new community to be the true Temple of Yahweh, reorienting all its symbols around himself as the site of Yahweh's promised return, the sacrifice for sin, and the restoration of Israel. But the restoration envisioned by Jesus would be one that came about through following a road that led to the cross, calling his followers upon the same path. As a "memorial" performance of *this* manner of deliverance, Jesus' Supper would also be the perpetuation of the "dangerous memory" of an unjust execution at the hands of corrupt officials and an indifferent empire.[46]

The eucharist, therefore, continually troubles the gathered church with an eschatological tension of being a martyr church on mission, filling up in itself what is lacking in the sufferings of Christ, and thereby thwarting any too easy embrace of present systems of governance. As such, it establishes the proper conception of the "secular" as "*saeculum*," a temporal notion

---

[45] The importance of the temple action here is noted by Neusner 1989.
[46] Much of the theoretical and theological analysis in what follows is inspired by Cavanaugh 1998:222-252 and 2002.

referring to this present world as both passing away in its provisional structures as well as remaining that which is to be redeemed within the bosom of the church.

Within the context of the Roman empire, this function of the eucharist took on other dimensions insofar as it conceived itself as the true sacrificial meal of which pagan feasts were only a false image. While Paul allows that meat sold openly at market could be permitted upon a Christian table, whatever its origin (1 Cor 8:1-6), he also decreed that it is not possible for a Christian to partake of the table of the Lord and the table of demons—to participate in the sacrificial feasts of the pagan *polis* and to gather in partnership as the body of Christ (1 Cor 10:14-21). Paul's use of the term "partnership" or "communion" here (*koinonia*) comes with cultic, economic, and political overtones, for within antique order local temples were not merely places of cultic ritual. Rather, they were thoroughly implicated within a complex network of social relations, literally defining space within the ancient *polis*, bound up with the privileges of citizenship and kinship, the stratification of political order, and forms of economic access.

Paul, of course, is no dualist and, in keeping with his Jewish creational monotheism, perceived now through Jesus, he recognized that all things exist through Jesus as Lord and messiah. Nonetheless, Paul introduced forms of moral reasoning, rooted in Jesus' Lordship and the practices of the Christian community as an integral community in itself, by which his hearers might wisely discern how to live as members of God's kingdom and household, making judgments within a world that, while under Jesus' Lordship, still resists God's reign. Indeed, the table of the Lord must serve as just such a place of discernment and judgment, manifesting the gathered Body of Christ in reconciled solidarity over against the world, thereby proclaiming the effective power of Jesus' death until he comes to judge.[47]

---

[47] On 1 Corinthians in its imperial context, see Horsley 2000:72-102. See also Leithart 1997b.

In this light, it is unremarkable that, not only does Paul proscribe involvement with the official cultic rites of pagan cities, he also forbids Christians from appealing to the pagan courts (1 Cor 6:1-6). This is not because such courts have no authority under God (we must presume), but because whatever legitimate authority those courts possess is already disclosed in a greater way within the church and, there, in light of eschatology and with eternal consequences (1 Cor 5:3-5; 6:2-3, 9). The eucharist, therefore, stands as a rite that encompasses the people of God both as a household and family gathered intimately at table and as a *polis* and nation assembled publicly at temple, thereby outwitting any absolute dichotomy between public space and private space.

But this eucharistic politics is one that knows no spatialized dualism of the natural and supernatural, rather functioning subjunctively in proclaiming and giving a foretaste of the ways things ought to be, against the remembrance of Jesus' death, a temporal movement, relating eschatology and history. As a ritual meal of eating and drinking, the eucharist forges a tie to this world as the place in which God's reign is realized, the transformation of this world in and through human action, and the establishment of peace.[48]

In particular we see a confluence of work and play, the mundane and the refined in the joining of bread with wine. Bread is basic sustenance but requires the establishment of human economy -- subsistence agriculture -- as well as the cessation of conflict and employment of human labor.[49] Wine, on the other hand, is a cup of playful celebration but requires some degree of technological sophistication, extended peace to age and mature, and the opportunity to relax and enjoy. The eucharist, therefore, projects a *communitas* in which such labor and celebration are valued, along with the peace to engage in them and the leisure to delight in them.[50] And insofar as the one and same Body of Christ is present wherever eucharist is made, the work of liturgy likewise undoes the logic of

---

[48] Leithart 1997b and Schmemann 1973:11-46.

[49] See Kass 1994:121-122.

[50] Empereur and Kiesling 1990:117-118.

center and circumference -- whether in terms of political, economic, social, or cultic centralization and stratification -- founding catholicity precisely in what is most local.

Conclusion

In these reflections, I have not offered anything near a comprehensive Christian politics. Nonetheless, I have attempted to underscore the ways in with the Gospel itself functions politically and implications drawn from that. And in some respects, I suggest, Christian politics consists first and foremost in living out that Gospel as church, enacting it authentically in community through the word and sacraments. Only by consciously engaging in such praxis and through continued reflection from within it, will it be possible to envision and move towards what that politics will mean for our particular lived conditions within neighborhoods and businesses, civic associations and civil government.

Still, several broad themes have emerged, I think, in the course of this discussion, and we would do well to bring them together here in summary. First, the Gospel of "Jesus is Lord" unravels any attempt to construct a Christian politics of "two kingdoms" in which the church and civil governments are set side-by-side as externally and extrinsically related orders. Rather the relationship is one of analogy, which, of course, presupposes a fixed distinction, without confusion, but also internal and intrinsic relations.[51]

---

[51] The echo of the Chalcedonian formulation of the two natures of Christ is intentional as it provides a helpful, though limited, analogy. According to that formulation, the human nature of Christ is united to the divine, but without any confusion with that divine nature. Nonetheless, the humanity of Jesus is enhypostatized by the single subject of the divine Son so that the humanity of Jesus is a perfect analogical revelation of deity. In an analogous manner the civil sphere must be seen as situated in relation to the church, without confusing the two spheres, but with the civil sphere analogically manifesting ecclesial "politics."

Second, ecclesial order and civil order thus do not occupy two different spaces, but two different *times*: the church having an eternal end, rooted in God's past saving acts in Christ, made present now in word and sacrament; the civil order having a temporal function within the present *saeculum*, ordained to continually pass away, though its treasures are carried in the bosom of the church into the eternal kingdom (Rev 21:24). Thus, rather than proving a threat to civil order, the church, as the true *polis* and kingdom, is the transcendent community before which immanent civil structures can be seen to have a reality and integrity quite apart from the exercise of force or the territorialization of space.

Third, these conceptions serve to relativize civil authority, situating it within and under the authority of God and his Christ. As a result, Christians cannot trust any human institution to ultimately secure our advantage, to be an object of final allegiance, or to sustain the missionary vocation of the church in the world. In light of the Gospel as the revelation of God's authority, justice, love, and universal concern, human authority is seen always to hold the potential to deify itself, to miscarry justice, to perpetuate violence, and to construct barriers.

Fourth, insofar as Christ is the model of truly human rule and the church is his Body, a renewed humanity, civil organization must come to be analogically fashioned in the image of the church, in a way that is appropriate for a temporal order and its ends, often exercising authority within communities consisting of both Christians and non-Christians. But there is no place here for a "common grace" politics that remains neutral to the claims of the Gospel, even with regard to the place of unbelievers within society, for it is precisely the Gospel that calls us to risk love even for enemies and to remain at peace with all people, as far as it is up to us (Rom 12:18). If anything is clear from Jesus' ministry, as a manifestation of God's justice, it is that the promises of God are not to be secured through violence.

This analogy, of course, can be pushed too far, though it has the ironic effect of suggesting that the Lutheran "two kingdoms" doctrine is incipiently Nestorian.

Finally, the politics engendered by ecclesial order provide a model for the analogous reconfiguring of social space in the ways suggested above: questioning the dichotomy of private and public spaces, disengaging centripetal forces and their relation to the peripheral and local, complicating homogenized space with a polymorphic organization of overlapping structures and authorities, and so on. These kinds of shifts would have significant implications for the exercise of civil authority, the shape of economic markets, the production and dissemination of culture, and so on. Clearly these implications suggest that the church stands as a witness to the possibility of a praxis that refuses the dichotomies offered by the modern: either nation-states or anarchistic turmoil, globalization or protectionism, unregulated capitalism or state socialism, and so on. But just *how* these binaries are to be overcome is left open and it is the church that must prove the site of resistance through a more self-conscious attempt to live out the Gospel as a counter-political community drawn together around word and sacrament.

Further implications might be drawn, but these few shall suffice. The Gospel, I have shown, is already politics and thus the church, as Augustine suggests, is the true *res publica* in light of which human community, politics, and justice is possible at all. And so, indeed, there is another king, this Jesus.

Bibliography

Alfoldy, Geza. *The Social History of Rome.* Trans. D. Braund and F. Pollock. London: Croom Helm, 1985.

Augustine. *De Civitatis Dei.*

Bartholomew, Craig, Jonathan Chaplin, et al (Eds.). *A Royal Priesthood: The Use of the Bible Ethically and Politically, A Dialogue with Oliver O'Donovan.* Grand Rapids: Zondervan, 2002.

Beard, Mary, and John North (Eds.). *Pagan Priests.* London: Duckworth, 1990.

Borg, Marcus J. *Conflict, Holiness, and Politics in the Teachings of Jesus.* Harrisburg: Trinity Press International, 1998.

Cantwell Smith, Wilfred. *The Meaning and End of Religion.* New York: Macmillan, 1962.

Cavanaugh, William T. *Theopolitical Imagination: Discovering the Liturgy as a Political Act in an Age of Global Consumerism.* London: T&T Clark, 2002.

-----. *Torture and Eucharist.* Oxford: Blackwell, 1998.

Certeau, Michel de. *The Mystic Fable.* Trans. Michael B. Smith. Chicago: University of Chicago Press, 1992.

Chenu, Marie-Dominique. *Towards Understanding St. Thomas.* New York: Regnery, 1964.

Clapp, Rodney. *A Peculiar People: The Church as Culture in a Post-Christian Society.* Downer Grove: InterVarsity Press, 1996.

Dumezil, Georges. *Archaic Roman Religion.* Trans. P. Krapp. Chicago: University of Chicago Press, 1970.

Elliott, Neil. *Liberating Paul: The Justice of God and the Politics of the Apostle.* Maryknoll: Orbis, 1994.

Empereur, James L., and Christopher G. Kiesling. *The Liturgy That Does Justice.* Collegeville: Liturgical Press, 1990.

Foucault, Michel. *The Order of Things: An Archaeology of the Human Sciences.* New York: Vintage, 1994.

Gaffin, Richard B. *Resurrection and Redemption: A Study in Paul's Soteriology.* Phillipsburg: Presbyterian and Reformed Publishing Company, 1987.

Garver, Stephen Joel. 2001. "A Brief Catechesis on Covenant and Baptism," website, La Salle University. <http://www.lasalle.edu/~garver/cateches.htm>

-----. 2000. "Mark's Jesus and Our Sufferings," website, La Salle University.
<http://www.lasalle.edu/~garver/markjesus.html>

-----. 1999. "Baptism in Matthew and Mark," website, La Salle University.
<http://www.lasalle.edu/~garver/NTbaptism.htm>

Georgi, Deiter. *Theocracy in Paul's Praxis and Theology.* Minneapolis: Fortress, 1991.

Gillespie, Michael Allen. *Nihilism Before Nietzsche.* Chicago: University of Chicago Press, 1994.

Hart, H. "The Coin of 'Render unto Caesar...'" in *Jesus and the Politics of His Day.* Ed. E. Bammel and C. F. D. Moule. Cambridge: Cambridge University Press, 1984.

Hauerwas, Stanley, and Charles Pinches. *Christians Among the Virtues.* Notre Dame: University of Notre Dame Press, 1997.

Hays, Richard B. *The Moral Vision of the New Testament: A Contemporary Introduction to New Testament Ethics.* New York: HarperCollins, 1996.

Hengel, Martin. *The Zealots: Investigations into the Jewish Freedom Movement in the Period from Herod I unto 70 AD.* Edinburgh: T&T Clark, 1989.

Horsley, Richard A. (Ed.). *Paul and Politics: Ekklesia, Israel, Imperium, Interpretation.* Harrisburg: Trinity Press International, 2000.

-----. *Paul and Empire: Religion and Power in Roman Imperial Society.* Harrisburg: Trinity Press International, 1997.

Jenkins, John. *Knowledge and Faith in Thomas Aquinas.* Cambridge: Cambridge University Press, 1997.

Jordan, Mark. *The Alleged Aristoteliansim of Thomas Aquinas*. Toronto: Pontifical Institute of Medieval Studies, 1992.

Kantorowicz, Ernst. *The King's Two Bodies: A Study in Medieval Political Theology*. Princeton: Princeton University Press, 1957.

Kass, Leon. *The Hungry Soul: Eating and the Perfecting of Our Nature*. New York: Free Press, 1994.

Kerr, Fregus. *After Aquinas: Versions of Thomism*. Oxford: Blackwell, 2002.

Leithart, Peter J. "Against Christianity: for the Church" in *Premise* Vol. IV.2. (1997a) <http://capo.org/premise/97/june/p9706 04.html>.

-----. "The Way Things Really Ought to Be: Eucharist, Eschatology, and Culture" in *Westminster Theological Journal* 59 (1997b): 159-76.

-----. *The Kingdom and the Power: Rediscovering the Centrality of the Church*. Phillipsburg: Presbyterian and Reformed Publishing Company, 1993.

Lubac, Henri de. *A Brief Catechesis on Nature and Grace*. San Francisco: Ignatius, 1984.

-----. *Mystery of the Supernatural*. Trans. Rosemary Sheed. New York: Crossroad Herder, 1998.

Milbank, John. *The Word Made Strange: Theology, Language, and Culture*. Oxford: Blackwell, 1997.

-----. *Theology and Social Theory: Beyond Secular Reason*. Oxford: Blackwell, 1993.Milbank, John, and Catherine Pickstock. *Truth in Aquinas*. New York: Routledge, 2001.

Montag, John, SJ. "Revelation: The False Legacy of Suarez" in *Radical Orthodoxy: A New Theology*. Ed. John Milbank, et al. London: Routledge, 1999.

Neusner, Jacob. "Money-changers in the Temple: The Mishnah's Explanation" in *New Testament Studies* 35 (1989):287-90.

Oakes, Peter. *Philippians: From People to Letter*. Cambridge: Cambridge University Press, 2001.

O'Donovan, Oliver. *Desire of the Nations*. Cambridge: Cambridge University Press, 1996.

O'Rourke, Fran. *Pseudo-Dionysius and the Metaphysics of Aquinas.* Leiden: E. J. Brill, 1992.

Pickstock, Catherine. *After Writing: On the Liturgical Consummation of Philosophy.* Oxford: Blackwell, 1998.

Polignac, Francois de. *Cults, Territory, and the Origins of the Greek City-State.* Trans. J. Lloyd. Chicago: University of Chicago Press, 1995.

Price, S.R.F. *Rituals and Power: The Roman Imperial Cult in Asia Minor.* Cambridge: Cambridge University Press, 1984.

Rahner, Karl. *Karl Rahner: Theologian of the Graced Search for Meaning.* Ed. Geffrey Kelly. Minneapolis: Fortress, 1992.

------. *Foundations of the Christian Faith: An Introduction to the Idea of Christianity.* Trans. Willima Dych. New York: Crossroad, 1978.

Saldarini, Anthony J. *Pharisees, Scribes, and Sadducees in Palestinian Society.* Grand Rapids: Eerdmans, 2001.

Sanders, E.P. *Judaism: Practice and Belief, 63 BCE - 66 CE.* Philadelphia: Trinity Press International, 1992.

Seifrid, Mark A. *Christ Our Righteousness: Paul's Doctrine of Justification.* Downers Grove: IVP, 2001.

Schindler, David L. *Heart of the World, Center of the Church: Communio Ecclesiology, Liberalism, and Liberation.* Grand Rapids: Eerdmans, 1996.

Schmemann, Alexander. *For the Life of the World: Sacraments and Orthodoxy.* Crestwood: St. Vladimir's Seminary Press, 1973.

Te Velde, Rudi. *Participation and Substantiality in Thomas Aquinas.* Leiden: E. J. Brill, 1995.

Wright, N.T. "Upstaging the Emperor" in *Bible Review* (February, 1998): 17, 47.

-----. *Jesus and the Victory of God.* Minneapolis: Fortress, 1992.

-----. *What Saint Paul Really Said.* Grand Rapids: Eerdmans, 1997.

Zaidman, Louise Bruit, and Pauline Schmitt Patel. *Religion in the Ancient Greek City.* Trans. Paul Cartledge. Cambridge: Cambridge University Press, 1989.

"The Kingdom of God is the supremacy of God in the sphere of blessedness. The connection between God's kingship and blessedness is partly of a generally eschatological character, partly of a specific kingdom-eschatological character. It is inherent in the eschatological conception of things that the final, perfect order of things shall also be the order of things productive of the supreme state of happiness."

Geerhardus Vos

Biblical Theology: Old and New Testaments

Christians, the State and Government

Cliff Bates

University of Warsaw
Poland

Human beings cannot escape from politics. This claim was made by Aristotle and never explicitly denied by scripture or by the noted Christian theologians. Given that Christians live in community with others and by their shared life with others cannot escape politics, is there a Christian understanding of the political community? But before we can answer this question we need to see how the political community understood in the contemporary age expressed and actualized. Today, when people speak of politics and political community, they speak in terms of the state. The state is the framework that shapes and defines the political life of human beings. Given this, is there then a Christian theory of the state? Or the better question is, perhaps, should there be a Christian theory of the state? If we look to the writings of Dietrich Bonhoeffer, one of the leading young Evangelical theologians whose life was cut short by the Nazis for his role in the plot to kill Hitler, the answer is no.

Dietrich Bonhoeffer argues that "The concept of the state is foreign to the New Testament. It has its origin in pagan antiquity. Its place is taken in the New Testament by the concept of government ('power'). The term 'state' means an ordered community; government is the power that creates and maintains order. The term 'state' embraces both the rulers and the ruled; the term 'government' refers only to the rulers."[1] Although I argue that Bonhoeffer wrongly attributes the concept of the state to the pagans, who, if one looks closely at, likewise do not speak of a state, yet Bonhoeffer's error here does not affect the power of this insight, that "The concept of the state is foreign to the New Testament." But why and how is the concept of the state foreign? In order to answer this we need to examine and understand the nature and history of the state.

What is the State?

The state is a product of modern political philosophy. The term "the state" is a creation of Machiavelli.[2] The modern state -- and its contemporary embodiment, the modern liberal state -- as we know it, although conceived by Machiavelli, is the child of Thomas Hobbes and continually developed by his intellectual forebears.[3] Although Hobbes does not explicitly define the state, it is

---

[1] Dietrich Bonhoeffer, *Ethics* (New York: MacMillian, 1954), 332.

[2] See Leo Strauss, *The Political Philosophy of Hobbes: Its Basis and Its Genesis*, trans. Elsa M. Sinclair (Chicago: University of Chicago Press, 1936), xv; Leo Paul de Alvarez (trans. and intro.), *Niccolo Machiavelli: The Prince* (Prospect Heights: Waveland Press, 1989), xii-xvii, xxxii-xxxiii; Harvey C. Mansfield, Jr., "On the Impersonality of the Modern State: A Comment on Machiavelli's Use of State," *American Political Science Review* 77 (1983) 849-857; J. H. Hexter, "Il Principe and lo Stato," *Studies in the Renaissance* IV (1956), 113-138; also, see Leo Strauss, *An Introduction to Political Philosophy: Ten Essays by Leo Strauss*, ed. Hilail Gildin (Detroit: Wayne State University Press, 1989), 39-55.

[3] See Thomas Hobbes, *Leviathan*, ed. Richard Tuck (Cambridge: Cambridge University Press, 1991).

nevertheless a conceptual product of this understanding of political community.[4]

The term Hobbes uses to specify the political community is the commonwealth. For Hobbes the commonwealth is the political entity within which human political behavior will be actualized. The real force of Hobbes' commonwealth must be understood in the expression of the sovereign power toward the subjects of the commonwealth. For Machiavelli the state is the articulated will of the prince -- an actual person. Hobbes takes this concept of the state and argues that it is not to be specifically the will of a prince or actual sovereign.

What is the sovereign power in Hobbes political thought? It is the articulated will of the social compact that gives legitimacy to the commonwealth. The reason the sovereign power arises out of a social contract is that, for Hobbes, a political community is not by nature, but is rather a humanly made construct. Thus, for Hobbes, political community is an artifact and, as such its political expression is the abstracted will of that which forms the political community.[5] Yet the term political community is no longer appropriate for the political entity that is being constructed; rather, such a community is referred to as "the body politic."

The body politic is a term or, more correctly a metaphor from Medieval political thought, which attempts to explain the relationship between a king and the realm he rules.[6] Hobbes' use of the term sovereign has long led readers to think he is speaking as if the sovereign will were a single human ruler, a king or a monarch. Hobbes is not referring to an actual human sovereign, but using the term as a metaphor to describe not a person but the embodied will of

---

[4] Strauss, *The Political Philosophy of Hobbes*, xv.

[5] See Leo Strauss, *Natural Right and History* (Chicago: University of Chicago Press, 1953); Pierre Manent, *An Intellectual History of Liberalism* (Princeton: Princeton University Press, 1994); Pierre Manent, "The Modern State," *In Lilla* (1994), 123-133.

[6] See Christine de Piza, *The Book of the Body Politic*, trans. and ed. Kate Langdon Forhan (Cambridge: Cambridge University Press, 1994); Ernst Kantorowicz, *The King's Two Bodies* (Princeton: Princeton University Press, 1957).

that which authorizes the body politic. The sovereign is thus no longer the body of the sovereign, i.e., the king or prince, but the abstracted will of the whole body politic.

The notion of the state is further developed along Hobbesian lines by both Rousseau, who shows how not only the state is a product of human construction but also of human rationality, and by Kant, who (1) shows that all moral action is an act of the will -- e.g., the categorical imperative, rather than an outcome of natural predisposition and (2) makes explicit that the state is a disembodied will. Thus, the modern state is no longer understood as the articulated will of any specific ruler, but rather the collective will of a whole of society it represents.

The concept of the modern state reaches its intellectual peak in Hegel's articulation of it. The history of the concept of the state entails a rejection of classical (i.e., that of the Greek and Roman) political thought's understanding of political community as a natural condition (this is to say environment or habitat) for human beings. Rather, "the state" offers a human construct that is nothing but the disembodied will of the body politic. But it does have a will and that will is the collective force underlying the legitimacy of its political rule. But if the state has a will, are we to understand it as a moral person? This is a question that has haunted modern political thought following Kant and Hegel.

Again, the concept of the state is one that was not developed until the Renaissance[7] and was not a intellectual concept at the time when either scripture was written or the Christian church founded. The state is an artificial construct, which represents the disembodied will of the body politic, whereas the polis (the city), which was the Classical concept of the political association, is a natural form of human association, that exists wherever man share a common life together. There is no human community without the polis, so Aristotle argues, and when a human being is outside the polis he is either a beast or a god.

---

[7] See Mansfield and de Alvarez, xiii-xviii.

The Political Entities before the State: The Tribe, the Empire, and the Polis.

In lieu of the state, the classical world spoke of the city (the polis). The concept of the polis came to light in Greek civilization and its development does suggest the invention of politics by the Greeks as Christian Meier in his book, *The Greek Discovery of Politics*, argues. The polis was a mean, a balance between empire and the tribe. Before the coming to be of the polis, human political and social organization fell between the rule of the tribe or the hegemonic empire.

Let us first look at the tribe. The tribe was based on kinship and blood, but it allowed for a great diversity of types and championed the freedom of its members and itself. The tribe has a hard time with those outside of it and membership in it is based on kinship and by blood, thereby making the inclusion of those outside the kin group or the tribe highly problematic. Another deficiency of the tribe is that it offered no development of arts, a written language, a literary culture, public buildings and monuments, etc., which is to say it lacks civilization. This occurs because the tribe's simple structure has its hands full dealing with the life and death issues of survival. Thus, the tribe, while being governed by the principle of freedom, in order to maintain that freedom and individualization, it must sacrifice the principle of civilization.

Now let us turn to the empire. The empire is a form of universal hegemonic rule that transcends blood or kin group. In fact an empire often unifies many different tribes and/or peoples. And to solidify that rule, it creates culture, language, literature, etc., that is to say it creates a civilization. But although empire creates and furthers civilization, it does so at the expense of heterogeneity and thus freedom of its members.

Now comes the polis. It is a middle ground between empire and tribe. The polis seeks to balance the principle of freedom with the benefits of civilization. It embraces the concept of heterogeneity in that there are a great variety of them. Yet it transcends the tribe in that membership in it is not founded in ties of kinship or blood.

The polis was the political community, the natural habitat for humans, which allowed human beings to fulfill their political natures. The polis was merely the given political community, and what governed and shaped any particular polis was its regime, which was the ruling body within that political community. The regime would shape the polis. It would shape the polis in that the regime gave the polis a particular form, a particular shape.

What is a regime, one may ask? A regime is the ruling element with a political community; it is those people who have authority in that city. These rules, justify their rule by making a claim about the just, i.e., they argue that their rule advances a particular understanding of justice. Thus the regime also attempts to define the values and beliefs of a community, especially in regard to the issue of justice and the good. Because there are different elements within a city that can rule, there exist a great variety of regimes. And when one ruling element replaces another that city has a change in regime, which is understood as a revolution. Oddly it was just when the polis recently ceased to be politically relevant that the Christian Church came into being.

Political Reality at the Foundation of the Christian Church

This history of the concept of the states shows us its wholly modern character. The very concept of the state was not present at the time scripture nor the Christian Church was founded. Rather political reality that confronted the Apostles was that of a cosmopolitan hegemonic empire, that came to exist out of the political crisis that ended the Roman Republic. The Roman Republic took the evolution of the political concept of the "city" (i.e., polis) and expanded it, universalized it. Rome became the universal city, and the Romans (albeit not always) gave the title of Roman citizen to those it conquered.

It could be argued that the classical political system of the polis died or ceased to be politically relevant with the victory of Phillip of Macedon over the Greeks. His son, Alexander, took the unity of the Greeks made possible by his father's victory over the independent Greek cities, and conquered Persia and created a unified Hellenistic Empire under his rule. This unified Hellenistic Empire died with him; what survived was the hegemonic rule of the various parts of this Empire under the rule of Alexander's generals. As these kingdoms squabbled with each other over access to trade routes to the East, the Power of Rome asserted itself in the Mediterranean. Rome expands due to fear and security and sooner or later it finds itself in charge of a large empire. And because possessing that empire led to conflict among the political elites, that conflict led to the end of the republic and the hegemonic rule of first three men and then later one man, Caesar and his successors. Enter Christianity.

What is interesting here is that although differing in principle and the goal each seeks to achieve, empire, tribe and polis are similar in that what defines them and what governs them is their rulers. The empire, the tribe and the polis, each is defined by their rulers. And their ruler is a person or set of persons. Now as we noted earlier, this is not true for the concept of the state, because the very state itself is an artificial person in that it is the collective will of the people who form it. But in forming the state, human being become like God, in that they create (not procreate) a moral being. This very fact should make the Christian think twice about the state, as Christians worry about cloning, abortion, and other issues of life and death.

Christians and the State

Christianity and Christians have no place for the concept of the state. The very concept of the State is highly problematic for the Christian. Why? Because the idea of the state states that the citizen must and should subsume his will to that of the collective will of the state, whereas scripture teaches us that the Christian should bound his will to God and to God alone; to do otherwise would lead us away from God and to our ultimate destruction.

In looking at the nature and logic of the state Christians will discover other troubling issues. One of them is that, the state, being the collective will of the society that forms it, allows its members to achieve and obtain the very good things and benefits they desire but by their own individual actions or natures are not able of obtaining. The state is created by man to secure the goods that nature, i.e., the realm of creation, gives human beings to desire but does not simply provide them with. By surrendering their will to this collective will, the person discovers that he or she is finally able to order and needed framework by which they can obtain what they desire. Thus the state becomes the benefactor of man and becomes the benefactor because neither nature nor its Creator cares enough about humans to provide for their needs. But Scripture tells us that the only true benefactor of man is God and that He does indeed provide for our needs and concerns. Scripture also teaches us that when we do not acknowledge God as our sole true benefactor but rather acknowledge others over him we are in error and that error only leads to evil and to our own destruction. The concept of the state is thus a substitute for God and anything that seeks to take the place of God is something Christians need to avoid. But can the Christian return to the less dangerous concept of the polis, the city? With any desire to return to using the concept of the city we are faced with immense difficulties. First and foremost, we no longer speak in our political speech of the city or understand it to be a self-defined political community but rather an urban center. And those who teach and understand political thought inform us that there is no return to the polis and that such longing for the return to the polis has brought nothing but great human evil and suffering. They assert that the modern state is here to stay. But can a Christian be content with this? The answer to this is no. A Christian cannot be at home or comfortable with the state.

But does this not make Christianity anarchistic? No. We are told by scripture to obey our rulers and our governors. Why? Because, God has given them authority over us. Scripture is very clear here, God has set over us rulers who are to govern us and to rule over us and to punish us when we do injustice and act lawlessly (Romans 13: 1-8). This does not mean that we blindly have to obey our rulers, especially when they act unjustly, or their rule is clearly evil and offers no room for justice or righteousness. Thus scripture does speak of government and here Bonhoeffer has something to teach:

> Government is divinely ordained authority to exercise worldly dominion by divine right. Government is deputyship for God on earth. It can be understood only from above. Government does not proceed from society, but it orders society from above. If it is exegetically correct to regard it as an angelic power, this would still serve only to define its position between God and the world. Only the concept of government, and not the concept of the state, can have a theological application.[8]

Thus when we seek to understand politics, we need to understand the concept of government and not the concept of the state.

Government and the Christian

Bonhoeffer argues that there are three bases of government: (1) in the nature of man; (2) in sin; and (3) in Christ.[9] Government is based in the human nature, that man being a political creature creates a habitat that allows for the fulfillment of that political

---

[8] Bonhoeffer, 332-333.
[9] Bonhoeffer, 333-338.

nature.[10] As mentioned above the classical world understood the natural habitat to the polis, the city. But, as Bonhoeffer notes, "for the New Testament the polis is an eschatological concept; it is the future city of God, the new Jerusalem, the heavenly society under the rule of God."[11] Yet this is to a degree also true of the classical Greeks, in that they spoke of the good polis, as defined by the best regime, an ideal which all polises fall short of and thus are measured by. The difference between the classical understanding and the scriptural understanding is that the former is founded and grounded only in nature and being an ideal is unlikely to come into being, but the latter is the promise of God and He has already established it and strives to and will eventually establish that kingdom on earth. This view of government is one founded in the Ancient world and at the early foundations of the Christian Church and forms of it remains today in a abridged form.[12]

Government is also founded upon sin. Bonhoeffer says this is the insight into government and political community stressed by the Reformation, which placed the origin of government in the fall of man.[13] He says, the reformer assert that:

> It was sin that made necessary the divine institution of government. The sword which God has given to government is to be used by it in order to protect man against the chaos which is caused by sin. Government is to punish the criminal and to safeguard life. Thus a reason is provided for the existence of government both as a coercive power and as the protector of an outward justice.[14]

---

[10] Here, I deviate from Bonhoeffer in that he attributes to the Greeks the concept of the state and view the polis as a form of the state. Given what I have argued above, this is not so. But Bonhoeffer's point that government is founded in human nature is a view upheld by the Greeks, the point he is trying to make is none the less correct, albeit how he expresses it is fundamentally incorrect.

[11] Bonhoeffer, 332.

[12] Bonhoeffer, 333-334.

[13] Bonhoeffer, 335.

[14] Bonhoeffer, 335.

There is therefore a natural tendency to understand government as coming out of either the commands of justice or the holding of power and thus coming not from above but from below, something made and established by man, for man. This understanding is wrong in that, as Bonhoeffer states, it fails to perceive that political community "is not a consummation of creaturely characteristics but an institution of God which is ordained from above."[15] God may permit society, culture, and forms of political society, but only "government is actually established and ordained by God Himself." He continues,

> People, culture, social organization, etc., are of the world. Government is order in the world, an order which bears the authority of God. Government is not itself of the world, but of God. On this basis the notion of the Christian state is also untenable; for the state possesses its character as government independently of the Christian character of the persons who govern. There is government also among the heathen.[16]

There can be no Christian state, or more correctly a Christian government, in that government is in itself a gift and creation from God and not man, and all government, even the government over non Christians, is still of God and serves God.

Finally, government is based in Christ in that not only sharing in common with all created things and beings its dependence upon Christ as its mediator, its creator, its goal and purpose (to serve Him), its ruler (in that Christ possesses all power in heaven and on earth), its savor and redeemer, but it also has a special relationship. That special relation, Bonhoeffer says, is five fold. (1) Christ was crucified with its permission. (2) It acknowledged and openly

---

[15] Bonhoeffer, 335.
[16] Bonhoeffer, 336.

declared Christ's innocence. (3) By letting Christ to be crucified, it fell to the pressure of the people, it failed to exercise its proper authority and function, but this failure is not a condemnation of the office but merely the faulty discharge of the office. (4) Christ submitted to it, although he reminded it that its power comes not from human will but from God.[17] (5) With these thing Christ "showed that government can only serve Him, precisely because it is a power which comes down from above, no matter whether it discharges it office well or badly. Both in acquitting Him of guilt and in delivering Him up to be crucified, government was obliged to show that it stands in the service of Jesus Christ."[18] Thus as he says "government serves Christ no matter whether it is conscious or unconscious of this mission or even whether it is true or untrue to it."[19] He continues, "If it is unwilling to fulfill this mission, then, through the suffering of the congregation, it renders service to the witness of the name of Christ. Such is the close and indissoluble relation of government to Christ. It cannot in either case evade its task of serving Christ. It serves Him by its very existence."[20] Thus, government is Christ's tool, even when it is in the hands of the ungodly. Understood in this light, we see that Scripture supports only a concept of government and how that concept is to be understood. We also have seen that the concept of the "state" is incompatible with an understanding of creation set forth in scripture. But would the establishment of a Christian state change this? Let us examine this question.

The Impossibility and Undesirability of a "Christian" State

As mentioned above the very idea of the state suggests the existence of a disembodied will that guides the subjects of society. The

---

[17] Bonhoeffer, 337-338.
[18] Bonhoeffer, 338.
[19] Bonhoeffer, 342.
[20] Bonhoeffer, 342.

danger for the Christian is to subject oneself to a will that is not the will of God. Does this problem resolve itself with the establishment of a "Christian" state? This leads to two issues: (1) the nature of the state and its lack of support in scripture and (2) concept of a Christian state. The former issue was addressed earlier and the initial response to the latter is that the lack of a scriptural support seems to undermine any basis for a Christian state. But let us examine more closely the latter issue of the possibility of a Christian state.

Bonhoeffer's understanding of government, as sketched out above, suggests the very idea of a "Christian" state is an ultimately dangerous concept. It is dangerous in that it fails to recognize that Christ's lordship is universal and extends over all creation, not merely over those who call themselves Christians. Christ is lord of all, both Christians and non-Christians.

The idea of a Christian state is also dangerous in that it may frustrate the Church, which is the body of Christ, in fulfilling its duty to reconcile the world back to God through Christ. It frustrates the Church by establishing a Manichean dichotomy, one that separate God from the world, the Christian from the non-Christian, and the good and righteous from the evil and the wicked. Such a view establishes two realms that are distinct and unbridgeable. Such a view trivializes God's sovereignty over all creation and suggests limits to God's authority.

The advocacy of a Christian commonwealth or state also runs the risk of legitimizing the exercise of the greatest evils and unrighteousness in the name of Christ and in doing so blasphemes against the perfectly just and righteous God. The concept of a Christian state also could mask evil rulers who seek to neutralize opposition to his rule by baptizing it. This is what happened in Germany under the rule of Hitler and the Nazis. The Hitler regime sought to neutralize the Christian opposition to its, by co-opting Christianity and making it his servant. Understanding what Hitler and his regime was up to in creation of the so-called "German Christians," led Bonhoeffer and others to oppose the Hitlerian regime. Their stand is put forth clearly for the whole world to see in the Barmen Declaration, which argues that the separation of Christian Church and human government is essential for the good of both and is clearly the will of God as understood by the teaching of Christ. Thus, the establishment of a Christian state is fundamentally undesirable in that it tends to establish an ungodly rule that dishonors God and leads its members away from what he wills for them. The undesirability of a Christian state leads to the view that since only what is desirable (i.e., that which leads to the fulfillment and healthy advancement of the human condition) is natural in existence. And what is not desirable cannot be, even though things may claim to be them, yet their claim is vain and false. So there cannot be a Christian state.

Although there cannot be a Christian state or commonwealth, there can be Christian rulers. But the fact that Christian are ruling (or are not ruling) does little to change the fact that government is creation of God and hence a gift to mankind, which cannot but carry out the providential role that it was created to fulfill. From this point of view, the very nature of government indicates the existence of Christian ruler is only an issue of optimality and not a question of legitimacy for the Christian. So, yes, Christians should seek to bring about what God wills, as made evident in scripture, and they should even engage in political life, but they should not seek to establish a Christian state, one that will established God's will. Doing this is in vain, since God's will is not established or brought to be by the act of man but by God himself though the instruments of his own choosing, which government, including secular government, is one.

Bibliography

Bloom, Allan (Trans. and Ed.). *The Republic of Plato.* New York: Basic Books, 1968.

Bonhoeffer, Dietrich. 1954. *Ethics.* New York: Macmillan, 1954.

de Alvarez, Leo Paul (Trans. and Intro.). *Niccolo Machiavelli: The Prince.* Prospect Heights: Waveland Press, 1989.

de Piza, Christine. *The Book of the Body Politic.* Tr. and Ed. Kate Langdon Forhan. Cambridge: Cambridge University Press, 1994.

Hexter, J. H. "Il Principe and lo Stato." *Studies in the Renaissance* IV (1956): pp.113-138.

Hobbes, Thomas. *Leviathan.* Ed. Richard Tuck. Cambridge: Cambridge University Press, 1991 [1651].

Kant, Immanuel. *Kant: Political Writings.* Ed. Hans Reiss. Cambridge: Cambridge University Press, 1991.

Kantorowicz, Ernst. *The King's Two Bodies.* Princeton: Princeton University Press, 1957.

Lilla, Mark (Ed.). New *French Thought: Political Philosophy.* Princeton: Princeton University Press, 1994.

Lord, Carnes (Trans. and Ed.). *Aristotle, The Politics.* Chicago: University of Chicago Press, 1984.

Manent, Pierre. *An Intellectual History of Liberalism.* Princeton: Princeton University Press, 1994..

-----. "Christianity and Democracy." Trans. Daniel Mahoney and Paul Seaton. *Crisis: Part I* (January, 1995): pp. 40-44; and *Part II* (February, 1995): pp. 42-48.

-----. "The Contest for Command." In Mark Lilla (1994): pp. 178-185.

-----. "The Modern State." In Mark Lilla (1994): pp. 123-133.

-----. *Tocqueville and the Nature of Democracy.* Savage: Roman and Littlefield, 1996.

Mansfield Jr., Harvey C. "On the Impersonality of the Modern State: A Comment on Machiavelli's Use of Stato." *American Political Science Review* 77 (1983): pp. 849-57.

Meier. Christian. *The Greek Discovery of Politics.* Cambridge: Harvard University Press, 1991.

Strauss, Leo. *An Introduction to Political Philosophy: Ten Essays by Leo Strauss.* Ed. Hilail Gildin. Detroit: Wayne State University Press, 1989.

-----. *Natural Right and History.* Chicago: University of Chicago Press, 1953.

-----. *On Tyranny. The Revised and Expanded Edition.* Eds. Victor Gourevitch and Michael S. Roth. New York: The Free Press, 1991.

-----. *The City and Man.* Chicago: University of Chicago Press, 1978.

-----. *The Political Philosophy of Hobbes: Its Basis and Its Genesis.* Trans. Elsa M. Sinclair. Chicago: University of Chicago Press, 1936 [1962].

-----. *What is Political Philosophy? And Other Studies.* Chicago: University of Chicago Press, 1988 [1959].

"Whoever gives even moderate attention to human affairs and to our common nature, will recognize that if there is no man who does not wish to be joyful, neither is there any one who does not wish to have peace. For even they who make war desire nothing but victory -- desire, that is to say, to attain to peace with glory. For what else is victory than the conquest of those who resist us? And when this is done there is peace. It is therefore with the desire for peace that wars are waged, even by those who take pleasure in exercising their warlike nature in command and battle. And hence it is obvious that peace is the end sought for by war. For every man seeks peace by waging war, but no man seeks war by making peace. For even they who intentionally interrupt the peace in which they are living have no hatred of peace, but only wish it changed into a peace that suits them better."

St. Augustine

The City of God

The Reformed Theocrats:
A Biblical Theological Response

Lee Irons

The Upper Register
California, USA

In this essay I intend to sketch a biblical theological argument against a theocratic view of "church and state" -- a view held by many Reformed fundamentalists and some of the smaller Reformed denominations. "Theocracy" must first be defined. Typically, it is understood to be a form of political government under the direct control of priests or clergy who claim to be authoritative representatives of God or some divine being (or beings). On this definition the ancient kingdom of Israel would not have been a theocracy, since the priestly office and the kingly office were clearly distinguished.

A better definition would be a form of political government in which (a) the civil authority confesses, in its official and civil capacity, commitment to a religious system of belief, (b) such confession being understood as necessary to the civil power's rightful authority, and (c) thus entrusting to the civil power the duty of enforcing that religious system of belief in the public realm. (What forms such enforcement takes may vary from extreme intolerance of alternative expressions of religious belief and practice, to a high degree of religious tolerance as long as citizens do not engage in treasonous attempts to undermine the state's official religious character.)

Theocratic principles of civil government may take a wide variety forms, and in fact have historically been the dominant mode of civil government throughout human history. There is nothing that prevents theocratic principles from being applied in any number of political and economic systems -- including dictatorships, absolute or constitutional monarchies, republican states, capitalist or socialist democracies, and so on. Theocracy in itself does not specify the form in which civil authority is exercised, or the extent to which it is based on the popular beliefs of the majority. For example, it is theoretically possible -- given the presence of a large enough of a majority of Americans, and the ratification of three fourths of the states -- for the Constitution to be amended so as to require all federal employees to be practicing Muslims, to include the confession, "There is no God but Allah and Mohammed is his prophet," in the oath of office for President and all other elected officials, and to prohibit public funds from being used to promote the teaching of any other religious viewpoint. The United States would then become a theocracy, but one that was instituted by democratic means (and which could, presumably, by de-instituted by the same means).[1]

---

[1] This hypothetical is an illustration of the oft-noted "tyranny of the majority." When Christian theocrats vociferously object that they are pursuing their political agenda by democratic means, their protests do little to reassure us. Meredith G. Kline remarks, "Queried about their goal of theocratic top-down domination of humanity, they tend to divert attention to the bottom-up process proposed for attaining it: likely victims of the contemplated purge are reassured that their Christian friends are going to vote for it all-nice-and-democratic-like." Review of *Dominion Theology: Blessing or Curse? An Analysis of Christian Reconstructionism*, by H. Wayne House and Thomas Ice, in *Journal of Church and State* 31 (Autumn 1989), 577-78.

In addition to "theocracy," another key term begs for definition -- and that is "fundamentalism." The Reformed theocrats who are the critical focus of this essay are a tiny group possessing little real political power. Thus, their theocratic aspirations are unlikely to be implemented in the near or distant future in a culturally diverse and religiously pluralistic nation like the United States. What, then, fuels their energy? The answer to this question lies in the sociological phenomenon of fundamentalism.

Fundamentalism exists within a wide spectrum of religious communities and is not to be equated with the specifically Protestant variety that rose in the United States during the fundamentalist-modernist controversy of the 1920s. However, that terminological polarity between fundamentalism and modernism is a useful conceptual scheme as long as it is not restricted to the cultural and theological split within American Protestantism. As a broader religious phenomenon fundamentalism is essentially a reaction against modernity and the perceived secular drift of western society. The media would like us to believe that fundamentalists are uneducated, poor, and from the backwaters of the earth untouched by modernity. But all varieties of fundamentalism (as a broader psychological and sociological phenomenon) flourish in constant reaction to modernity, and are in some ways created by it. Thus fundamentalism is most attractive to those with religiously conservative values who feel surrounded and besieged on all sides by a hostile, secular dominant culture. Without this sense of alienation from a culturally dominant secularism, fundamentalism would collapse into privatized religious piety.

This observation is useful, because it shows the difference between fundamentalism and religious conservatism. The former is engaged in a war with a secular society, a war whose victory is defined in nothing less than the dislodgment of the secular powers-that-be and their replacement by a new social order that is in essential conformity with the dictates of their religious worldview. Non-fundamentalist religious conservatives, by contrast, may hold to the same religious values in their personal lives, families, and religious communities, but without the driving pursuit of cultural clout and political power. Those whose worldview demands that their religious values be given cultural and societal expression, but who lack the power to achieve that goal and who feel that their values are being continually eroded and assaulted by the dominant culture -- fit the classic fundamentalist profile to a T.

Due to this intermeshing of cultural, political, and religious factors, theocratic political ideals are often found among fundamentalists. Like the Islamic fundamentalists who exists as a subgroup within mainstream Islam, so there exists within American evangelicalism a significant segment of militant evangelicals (i.e., fundamentalists) who believe that the Christian religion provides more than a way of salvation for the individual, and that its values demand concrete expression not only in the community of fellow believers in the church, but in society as a whole. Among the fundamentalists there is a smaller sub-group who hold to the Reformed theology of John Calvin, John Knox, and the Puritan Westminster Confession of Faith. These Reformed theocratic fundamentalists are concerned to uphold the notion that Christianity is not a privatized religious experience but a comprehensive world and life view with implications for civil government and public policy.

The *God and Politics* Debate

Who are the Reformed theocrats? There are a number of ways to answer this question, but we can get our bearings by considering a volume titled, *God and Politics: Four Views on the Reformation of Civil Government*, edited by Gary Scott Smith. This book arose out of a conference held on June 2 and 3, 1987, titled, "Consultation on the Biblical Role of Civil Government," held at Geneva College in Beaver Falls, Pennsylvania. Over 100 conservative Reformed Christians were in attendance at the conference. The conference planners identified four major positions within the Reformed community with regard to the biblical teaching on civil government, and leading representatives of each view were invited to defend their position. The four views identified were: theonomy, principled pluralism, Christian America, and national confessionalism. The papers, as well as responses from other Reformed spokesmen, were published in book form in 1989 by Presbyterian and Reformed Publishing Company.[2]

The four views, in brief, may be summarized as follows:

Theonomy teaches that all the standing laws prescribed for Israel in the Mosaic Law are still binding today as a blueprint for socio-political ethics, unless explicitly rescinded by later revelation.

Principled pluralism is the view that the civil government should allow religious diversity within society and that Christians should adopt and promote public policy based on the biblical notion of social justice and concern for the poor. Of the four views represented at the conference, this was the only non-theocratic Reformed option on church and state given a platform.

Christian America holds that America used to be a Christian nation, founded on the basic morality of the Bible as summarized in the ten commandments, and that we ought to be politically active in seeking to restore America to that foundation.

National confessionalism asserts that not only individuals but entire nations have a duty to profess the Christian faith. When the Constitutional Congress created this nation, it failed to explicitly acknowledge the Kingship of Jesus Christ. Therefore, in contradistinction from the Christian America view, national confessionalism denies that America ever was a Christian nation. However, it agrees that it ought to be. The National Reform

---

[2] *God and Politics: Four Views on the Reformation of Civil Government*, ed. Gary Scott Smith (Phillipsburg: Presbyterian and Reformed Publishing Company, 1989). Hereafter cited as *GAP*.

Association[3] has proposed the following amendment to the Preamble of the Constitution in order to make America a Christian nation:

> We the people of the United States, humbly acknowledging Almighty God as the source of all authority and power in civil government, the Lord Jesus Christ as the Governor among the nations, and His revealed will as of supreme authority, in order to constitute a Christian government ... do ordain and establish this Constitution for the United States of America.[4]

Such a corporate confession of Christ as "the Governor" of the nations and of the Bible as the "supreme authority" would certainly qualify as theocratic. One national confessionalist in *God and Politics* candidly identifies his position: "I have always preferred to refer to myself as a 'Christian theocrat' rather than a theonomist."[5]

---

[3] The National Reform Association, based in Pittsburgh, PA, was founded in 1864 by Reformed theocrats, including many from the Reformed Presbyterian Church of North America, the American descendants of the Scottish covenanters. Recently, the NRA has been ramping up its political activism by means of "Operation Potomac," which involves regular visits with key Republicans in the Bush administration as well as the House of Representatives. For example, a recent visit to Washington, D. C., on April 25, 2001, is described as follows: "Concentration for this operation centered on the Department of Justice and the White House. In the morning our team met with Attorney General John Ashcroft's policy advisors wherein we discussed various issues, distributed copies of 'Explicitly Christian Politics' and 'Messiah the Prince' along with copies of 'The Christian Statesman' and a framed proclamation which outlines the NRA's positions for Christian civil government." NRA president Jeffrey Ziegler explains that these efforts "are but part of a total revitalization of the National Reform Association. When combined with state chapters, additional publications, media production, and the eventual inauguration of a legal lobbying arm, the NRA will once again become the driving force for an explicitly Christian vision of government" (from the NRA website, www.natreformassn.org).
[4] *GAP*, p. 189. Such an amendment was actually debated (and rejected) by the House of Representatives in 1874 and again in 1896.
[5] *GAP*, p. 69.

As you might imagine from this brief sketch, the spokesmen for three of the views found that they had much in common. Although differing among themselves on the application of the Mosaic judicial laws to modern society, on eschatological expectations, and on the question of whether America ever was a Christian nation to begin with, the advocates of theonomy, Christian America, and national confessionalism were united in their condemnation of principled pluralism. Without downplaying their differences, it is legitimate to call these three views *theocratic* since they all agree that the civil government ought not to be religiously neutral.

Further evidence of the underlying theocratic unity of these three views may be found in their respective responses to Bahnsen's theonomic essay. For example, H. B. Harrington wrote that he agreed with Bahnsen in many respects and expressed the "fervent desire that theonomists and national confessionalists will be able to consolidate their agreements and work out their disagreements at least to the degree that we will be able to cooperate fully with each other."[6] It turns out that these words were somewhat prophetic, for since the 1987 forum, the two groups (theonomists and national confessionalists) have developed an alliance. For example, the editor of *The Christian Statesman* (the journal of the National Reform Association) during much of the 1990s was Andrew Sandlin, who is also an editor of *The Chalcedon Report*, a theonomic journal founded by R. J. Rushdoony. And the current president of the National Reform Association since 1999 is Jeffrey Ziegler, a fervent theonomist who vigorously promotes theocratic political activism on a radio program that claims to be "one of the most provocative and evocative of its type."[7]

The advocates of Christian America are also fundamentally "on board" with this theocratic agenda. Kevin L. Clauson states in

---

[6] *GAP*, p. 68.

[7] According to the NRA website, Christian Statesman Radio is broadcast throughout Michigan, Indiana, Kentucky, western Pennsylvania, West Virginia, and parts of Canada (e.g., on WHK - 1220 AM - in Cleveland from 5:00 to 6:00 p.m. on a daily basis). Syndication of the program is being discussed.

his response to Bahnsen that the question of whether or not America ever was a Christian nation is not nearly as important as whether or not it should be one in the future. His position on the latter question is clear:

> America and other nations can be Christian if they adopt biblical laws in state, church, family, and all other entities and associations. We cannot trust man (individually or collectively); we must trust God and His immutable law. If civil magistrates will not apply the Old Testament law, then what will they apply? The law of man. If we will not be ruled by God, we will be ruled by tyrants.[8]

These words could very well have been written by Bahnsen himself without altering a single syllable.

In view of the substantial unity among "the theocratic triumvirate" (whose differences amount merely to the exegetical details of how to translate their vision into reality), it is somewhat surprising that only one non-theocratic alternative was represented in the book -- that of principled pluralism. And in this case the contribution by Gordon Spykman was not principially opposed to theocracy, lacked cogent exegetical and theological argumentation, and tended to focus on his own unique interests in the area of social welfare for the poor.

In this essay I set forth the case for a fifth view which was not represented at the conference, and which merited only one footnote.[9] This is what I call the biblical theological view. It has affinities with principled pluralism – as evidenced, for example, by the fact that it has also regularly provokes the wrath of Reformed theocrats. But this view is distinct enough from it to warrant

---

[8] *GAP*, p. 67.

[9] Bahnsen dismisses Meredith Kline's biblical theological understanding of civil government as a version of "the sacred-secular dichotomy" which Bahnsen laments as having recently "infected" the Reformed community. *GAP*, p. 22; also, cf. footnote 3 on that page.

separate treatment. Surely, if the rather fine distinctions among the other three views warranted separate treatment, then another biblical case for pluralism does too.

An uncrossable gulf lies between those views which advocate a self-consciously religious role for civil government and those views which advocate a religiously neutral role for the civil government. It is my goal in this essay to make that gulf clear and to attempt to persuade the reader that the biblical theological approach to the question of "church and state" is a more biblical option.

A Sample Theocratic Argument: Theonomy

In *God and Politics* the theonomic view is ably defended by Greg L. Bahnsen. For the purposes of this essay, I have chosen Bahnsen as my sample Reformed theocrat, since (in addition to R. J. Rushdoony and Gary North) Bahnsen is one of the well-known authors from the theocratic camp. The fundamental thesis of theonomy -- in spite of minor differences of interpretation among the leaders of the movement -- contains two prongs: (1) the Mosaic Law provides an unchanging, divinely-revealed standard for socio-political ethics, and (2) the civil government has a moral duty to conform its laws and actions to that unchanging standard. Concerning the first prong, I quote Bahnsen:

> We should presume that Old Testament standing laws continue to be morally binding in the New Testament, unless they are rescinded or modified by further revelation .... The general continuity that we presume with respect to the moral standards of the Old Testament applies just as legitimately to matters

of socio-political ethics as it does to personal, family, or ecclesiastical ethics.[10]

As to the second prong, Bahnsen states:

> Civil magistrates in all ages and places are obligated to conduct their offices as ministers of God, avenging divine wrath against criminals and giving an account on the Final Day of their service before the King of kings, their Creator and Judge.[11]

> Where do civil magistrates find the political dictates of God? Surely not in varying subjective opinions, personal urges, the human wisdom of some elite group, the majority vote, or even a natural revelation that is suppressed and distorted in unrighteousness.[12]

> In the exercise of their offices [civil] rulers are morally responsible to obey the revealed standards of social justice in the Old Testament law.[13]

Sometimes theonomists give the impression that these matters are simple and clear-cut; the only impediment is disobedience. But theonomists do not claim to have answers to all policy questions, and they recognize that much more work needs to be done in the area of interpreting the Mosaic Law and applying it to modern society. Bahnsen recognizes the hermeneutical challenge of applying laws given to an ancient agrarian society (Israel) to the modern nation-state with its technological advances. Nevertheless, the challenge is not inherently insurmountable and, in principle, all our modern social and political problems can be solved by the

---

[10] *GAP*, p. 24.

[11] *GAP*, p. 24.

[12] *GAP*, p. 31.

[13] Greg L. Bahnsen, *No Other Standard: Theonomy and Its Critics* (Tyler: Institute for Christian Economics, 1991). Hereafter cited as *NOS*.

straightforward methods of grammatical-historical exegesis and culturally sensitive biblical application.

It is illuminating from a comparative religious standpoint to note the parallels between theonomy and the religio-political ideals of the Islamist movement. Islamism, or Islamic fundamentalism, seeks the rule of the Shariah (Islamic law as defined by the various legal schools of Koranic interpretation) in all Islamic nations, and in principle the whole world. This movement is theocratic because it envisions a non-pluralistic society, the fundamental fabric of which is religious. According to Islamic fundamentalists, Islam demands concrete social and civil "incarnation." They claim that their sacred texts provide a blueprint for this ideal society that is both sufficient and comprehensive. It is thought to be sufficient, because the authority of the Koran and the Hadith does not need to be supplemented by human ideas, tradition, reason, science, or input from any other source of knowledge or experience. Comprehensive, because the Koran is believed to provide the principles necessary for the divinely authorized shaping of every area of life -- not only the personal religious and ethical life of the individual believer, family, or religious community (mosque), but that of society as a whole, in all of its complex operations and functions.[14] Approximately the same understanding of the role of the Bible as "a comprehensive world and life view" applies to theonomic fundamentalists, *mutatis mutandis*.

To illustrate how the theonomic viewpoint would be fleshed out in practice, if a nation were to adopt the theonomic platform, it is valuable to point out Bahnsen's response to the question of the application of the death penalty mandated in the Mosaic Law to those who are found guilty of engaging in homosexual acts.

> Paul says in Romans 1 that homosexuals know that
> what they are doing is worthy of death. He adds in 1

---

[14] For more on the origins and historical development of Islamic fundamentalism as a reaction to Islamic modernism, see "Islam Passes through the Shadows," chapter 20 in Ninian Smart, *The World's Religions*, 2nd revised ed. (Cambridge: Cambridge University Press, 1998).

Timothy 1 that the law is lawfully used when homosexuals are punished to restrain their activity .... Some people object, however, by saying that if you execute a homosexual then you have no chance to evangelize him. The same is true if you execute a murderer. But that is not for us to determine. If a person is going to be converted, he will be converted in God's due time. It is not for us to adjust the requirements of His law because we want to provide occasions for a person to repent.[15]

Another important implication of theonomy is that civil rulers must enforce the Christian religion and suppress alternative religious expressions deemed subversive of the state-protected Christian church. Bahnsen writes, appealing to the Reformed tradition:

The pluralism which was promoted and defended by our Reformed forefathers was not a civil tolerance which countenanced and protected all religions equally, but rather a civil tolerance for all branches and denominations within the circle of Christianity.[16]

He favorably quotes Puritan theologian John Owen (1616-1683) who stated:

The supreme magistrate, in a nation or commonwealth of men professing the religion of Jesus Christ, may and ought to exert his power, legislative and executive ... to forbid, coerce, or restrain such principles and practices as are contrary

---

[15] *GAP*, p. 266.
[16] *NOS*, p. 185.

to [the faith and worship of God] and destructive of them.[17]

To be fair, we must note that Bahnsen is careful to add the following qualifications. First, the civil power should not be exercised against unbelievers merely for their lack of faith in Christ, apart from criminal acts that might flow from that unbelief.[18] Bahnsen appeals to the uncircumcised stranger who dwelled within the borders of Israel, and who was allowed to exist unmolested even if he refused to participate in the religion of Israel. Thus unbelievers would not be persecuted or punished merely for their unbelief, or for refusing to profess faith, or for not attending church. Only *public* religious crimes, such as public acts of idolatry, false prophecy, public blasphemy, offering one's services as a medium -- would be punishable by the civil magistrate.[19] Religious crimes punishable by the civil power are "always public misdeeds as defined by God's revelation."[20]

Second, the civil power should not be exercised with respect to the affairs of the church, thus maintaining the distinction between church and state.[21] The civil magistrate is not competent to exercise the power of the keys of the kingdom, to exercise church discipline, to judge heretics, or to settle doctrinal disputes between different schools of Christian thought. It is a common misunderstanding to say that theonomy blurs the distinction between church and state. Such institutional distinctions are not violated, Bahnsen argues, when the magistrate exercises his authority to punish those who have committed religious crimes.

---

[17] *NOS*, p. 185. Bahnsen quotes Owen, "Two Questions Concerning the Power of the Supreme Magistrate About Religion and the Worship of God" (1659), in *The Works of John Owen* (vol. XIII), ed. William H. Goold (London & Edinburgh: Johnstone and Hunter, 1852), p. 509.

[18] *NOS*, p. 187.

[19] *NOS*, pp. 136, 174, 186.

[20] *NOS*, p. 175.

[21] *NOS*, p. 188.

The third qualification is that the morally proper way for Christians to seek to have these principles implemented in society today is not by the use of force or revolution, but by means of peaceful persuasion and education, gradual legal reform, and democratic mechanisms, all in dependence on the regenerating work of the Spirit.[22]   Thus Bahnsen answers   another common misconception of the theonomic thesis.

When the above qualifications and distinctions are observed, we must recognize that in the theonomist's ideal world, there would be a certain degree of religious liberty. There would be tolerance for non-Christians so long as they did not actively subvert the civil order by means of public acts of idolatry, and there would be toleration for all denominations of Christians. None of this would compromise the church-state distinction, or require Christians to use the sword to achieve their political goals.

In spite of these qualifications, theonomists insist that it is the magistrate's responsibility, indeed "his chief and supreme care and duty," to see to it that the true worship of God is protected and promoted in society, to prevent "the appointment of any thing inconsistent with it."[23]   So yes, theonomists believe in religious toleration of persons who keep their beliefs and practices to themselves and "in no way interfere with"[24] the true Christian religion!   But non-Christians would *not* be legally permitted to attempt to convert others to their religious beliefs, to publish any writings that attack Christianity, or in any way to exercise freedom of (religious) expression in the public arena.

Even professing Christians would not be permitted to publicly voice criticisms of the theocratic principles and foundation of the state. Non-theonomic Reformed Christians (like the author of this essay) who publicly promote their critique of theonomy would be a particular threat to a theonomic state, since their critique could well be deemed a "political defection from, or subversion of, the law

---

[22] *NOS*, p. 13; cp. *GAP*, p. 24-25.

[23] *NOS*, pp. 185f, again quoting John Owen, "Two Questions," pp. 510-11.

[24] *NOS*, p. 185.

order of ... society by renouncing its highest authority."[25] Bahnsen provides the theological justification for the persecution on non-theonomic Christians when he identifies their pluralistic viewpoint as idolatry:

> By contending that civil policy should not be based upon or favor any one distinctive religion or philosophy of life ... pluralism ultimately takes its political stand with secularism in refusing to "kiss the Son" and "serve Jehovah with fear." The pluralist approach transgresses the first commandment by countenancing and deferring to different ultimate authorities (gods) in the area of public policy ... a kind of "political polytheism." The Bible warns us how our ascended and supreme King, Jesus Christ, will react to political refusal to do homage to Him and to obey His law: He will become "angry [with a wrath already kindled] and you will perish in the way" (Ps. 2:12).[26]

Any theological-political viewpoint which provokes the wrath of the ascended King should logically be proceeded against by the King's earthly representative, the civil magistrate. If the theonomists were ever to succeed in gaining political ascendancy, the theonomic police would certainly seize this essay as irrefutable evidence of my political refusal to do homage to King Jesus, and I could potentially "perish in the way."

Reformed Roots of Theonomy

---

[25] *NOS*, p. 178.

[26] *GAP*, p. 30. Words in brackets are Bahnsen's.

Theocratic ideals of the civil government go all the way back to the decree of Theodosius in AD 380 which made Trinitarian Christianity (defined at the council of Nicea in AD 325) the official religion of the Roman Emperor. Such ideas continued throughout the Middle Ages and were reaffirmed by the magisterial reformation. In the British Isles, theocratic ideas held particular sway among the Reformed. The Westminster Confession (1646), authored by an assembly of about 100 Puritan theologians, affirms that it is the duty of the civil magistrate to enforce the Christian religion in the public sphere:

> The civil magistrate may not assume to himself the administration of the Word and sacraments, or the power of the keys of the kingdom of heaven: *yet he hath authority, and it is his duty, to take order, that unity and peace be preserved in the Church, that the truth of God be kept pure and entire, that all blasphemies and heresies be suppressed, all corruptions and abuses of worship and discipline prevented or reformed, and all the ordinances of God duly settled, administered, and observed* (WCF XXIII:3).

However, these views did not last long. In 1788 the American Presbyterian church as a corporate body self-consciously rejected its theocratic/establishmentarian heritage by revising the Confession to teach religious liberty and civil pluralism. The fact that the Confession itself was revised, rather than merely continuing the tradition of Presbyterian allowance of non-theocratic views of the civil magistrate (as had been done for about sixty years prior to the revision), suggests that this new, American, non-theocratic tradition was a unanimous, corporate conviction.

A couple of theocratic phrases were deleted, but the most extensive change was the drafting an (almost) entirely new third paragraph of chapter XXIII:

Civil magistrates may not assume to themselves the administration of the Word and sacraments; or the power of the keys of the kingdom of heaven; *or, in the least, interfere in matters of faith. Yet, as nursing fathers, it is the duty of civil magistrates to protect the church of our common Lord, without giving the preference to any denomination of Christians above the rest, in such a manner that all ecclesiastical persons whatever shall enjoy the full, free, and unquestioned liberty of discharging every part of their sacred functions, without violence or danger. And, as Jesus Christ hath appointed a regular government and discipline in his church, no law of any commonwealth should interfere with, let, or hinder, the due exercise thereof, among the voluntary members of any denomination of Christians, according to their own profession and belief. It is the duty of civil magistrates to protect the person and good name of all their people, in such an effectual manner as that no person be suffered, either upon pretence of religion or of infidelity, to offer any indignity, violence, abuse, or injury to any other person whatsoever: and to take order, that all religious and ecclesiastical assemblies be held without molestation or disturbance.*

These changes did not alter the fundamental Reformed or Calvinistic theology of the Westminster Confession, but they did constitute an about-face on the issue of theocracy.[27]   In the

---

[27] Bahnsen attempts to downplay the significance of the American revisions, claiming that it was merely an attempt to "clarify" the original Confession's stance on church-state relations, not an "intentional repudiation," although he wishes they had left it unchanged. *Theonomy in Christian Ethics* (Phillipsburg: Presbyterian and Reformed Publishing Company, 1984), pp. 541-44.   Gary North is more critical of the 1788 revisions and candidly expresses his opinion that the American Presbyterians "gutted" the original Confession and thus "moved forthrightly onto a

providence of God, the eighteenth century American Presbyterian church declared in no uncertain terms that it now found the theocratic views of its Reformed forefathers to be unbiblical and erroneous, and determined corporately to confess a more biblical approach.   This was the general consensus of the American Presbyterian position on church-state relations. It emerged after the Revolutionary era and continued relatively unchallenged until the rise of theonomy in the late 1960s.[28]

After the American Presbyterian revisions to the Confession, the revival of the theocratic tradition in the twentieth century may seem unexpected, but it is simply the Reformed version of the more general phenomenon of fundamentalism.   This Reformed fundamentalist-theocratic reaction was triggered by a sense of the erosion of the Judeo-Christian values that had hitherto shaped public morality and policy, by the rapid onslaught of a secularization process that took place in modern society throughout the twentieth century, and by the resultant loss of the cultural clout and political influence previously possessed by the evangelical community in the nineteenth century.[29]

The American Presbyterians of the post-Revolutionary era -- partly influenced by the changing attitudes toward church and state relations, and partly due to a sound biblical instinct concerning the spirituality of the church -- are to be applauded for amending the Confession to rid it of outdated theocratic elements. Nevertheless, the biblical case for their amending the Confession was not as fully articulated as it could have been. A full-orbed theological and exegetical rationale for the rejection of the idea of Christian theocracy did not emerge until the closing quarter of the twentieth

---

long road that leads into culturally muddled theology." *Theonomy: An Informed Response*, ed. Gary North (Tyler: Institute for Christian Economics, 1991), p. 344.

[28] Prior to theonomy, few Presbyterians in the United States espoused theocracy, except for the tiny Reformed Presbyterian Church of North America (Covenanters).

[29] George M. Marsden narrates the rise of this 19th century pan-evangelical cultural influence (which he calls "the benevolent empire") in *The Evangelical Mind and the New School Presbyterian Experience* (New Haven: Yale University Press, 1970).

century by Reformed biblical theologians in response to the revival by Reformed theocrats of the anachronistic ideal of Christendom.

A Biblical Theological Response

The term "biblical theology" has various meanings. Its most common usage is to describe the exegetical methodology that seeks to determine the theology espoused by the biblical authors, as distinct from dogmatic theology which seeks to guide the church's contemporary formulation. In this essay "biblical theology" refers to a specific tradition within that general methodology. The father of Reformed biblical theology is Geerhardus Vos (1862-1949), professor of Old Testament at Princeton Theological Seminary. The tradition of Vos has been carried on at Westminster Theological Seminary by such theologians as John Murray, Edmund P. Clowney, and Richard Gaffin.

The most important biblical theological developments since Vos -- particularly in relation to the development of a sound biblical critique of theonomy -- have been produced by Meredith G. Kline. In an important and often-cited article that appeared in *The Westminster Theological Journal* in 1978, Kline sets forth a biblical theological argument against theonomy (which he refers to as "the Chalcedon theory").[30] The arguments presented there will form the basic structure of the following precis, supplemented along the way by other writings by Professor Kline, as well as by other Reformed biblical theologians in the Vos tradition.

(1) The redemptive historical purpose of the Mosaic Law

---

[30] Kline, "Comments on an Old-New Error," *WTJ* 41 (1978), 172-89. Founded by R. J. Rushdoony in 1965, the Chalcedon Foundation is a Christian Reconstructionist/theonomic educational institute which publishes *The Chalcedon Report* (www.chalcedon.edu).

The most obvious biblical error that lies at the heart of theonomy is its decovenantalized conception of the Mosaic Law. Theonomy treats the Mosaic Law given to Israel as universally binding on all nations, even though they were not originally party to Israel's covenant with Yahweh. "Plainly, the duties of a given covenant are only obligatory on those who are parties to the covenant. For Theonomy, however, all peoples in all times are obliged to these duties."[31] Because of God's special act of divine redemption displayed at the exodus, and the subsequent special revelation at the giving of the Law on Mount Sinai covenant, Israel was constituted God's people with a national constitution (the Mosaic Law). Lacking such direct divine intervention in the form of a nation-forming divine redemption accompanied by special, covenantal revelation, the nations of the earth outside of Israel have no right to place themselves under the specific obligations of the Law given at Sinai. Kline writes:

> While the Bible says Israel was separated from the other nations to be a unique, holy kingdom, Bahnsen says that God's kingdom Israel was just another civil government.... To accept the Chalcedon theory, one would have to read the biblical record [of Israel's divine election, special vocation, and redemptive deliverance] as though it were not the history of the particular kingdom of Israel but an historicized myth about Everynation.[32]

By treating the Mosaic Law as a generic civil code for Everynation, theonomy must suppress the clear teaching of Scripture concerning the exclusively redemptive historical purpose of the Mosaic Law. According to the teaching of Paul, the Law -- with its punishments and its earthly blessings and curses -- was "a ministry of condemnation" (2 Cor. 3:9), a harsh disciplinarian to prepare us

---

[31] T. David Gordon, "Critique of Theonomy: A Taxonomy," *WTJ* 56 (1994), 23-43.

[32] Kline, "Comments," p. 178.

for the coming of Christ. Now that Christ has been born under the Law and become a curse for us, the Mosaic Law has served its purpose in redemptive history.

Galatians 3:17—4:7 What I am saying is this: the Law, which came four hundred and thirty years later, does not invalidate a covenant previously ratified by God, so as to nullify the promise. 18 For if the inheritance is based on law, it is no longer based on a promise; but God has granted it to Abraham by means of a promise.

19 Why the Law then? It was added because of transgressions, having been ordained through angels by the agency of a mediator, until the seed would come to whom the promise had been made .... For if a law had been given which was able to impart life, then righteousness would indeed have been based on law. 22 But the Scripture has shut up everyone under sin, so that the promise by faith in Jesus Christ might be given to those who believe. 23 But before faith came, we were kept in custody under the law, being shut up to the faith which was later to be revealed. 24 Therefore the Law has become our tutor to lead us to Christ, so that we may be justified by faith. 25 But now that faith has come, we are no longer under a tutor ....

4:1 Now I say, as long as the heir is a child, he does not differ at all from a slave although he is owner of everything, 2 but he is under guardians and managers until the date set by the father. 3 So also we, while we were children, were held in bondage under the elemental things of the world. 4 But when the fullness of the time came, God sent forth His Son, born of a woman, born under the Law, 5 so that He might redeem those who were under the Law, that we might receive the adoption as sons. 6 Because you are sons, God has sent forth the Spirit of His Son into our hearts, crying, "Abba! Father!" 7 Therefore you are no longer a slave, but a son; and if a son, then an heir through God.

The Law has clear temporal boundaries, both a historical beginning and a historical terminus. It came 430 years *after* the Abrahamic promises. And it was "added *until* the Seed should come.... Now that faith has come, we are no longer under the pedagogue (i.e., the Law)." From the outset God gave it with the coming of Christ in view. He gave the Law to provide the proper covenantal context in which Christ would accomplish our redemption. Kline explains:

> In accordance with the terms of his covenant of works with the Father he was to come as the second Adam in order to undergo a representative probation and by his obedient and triumphant accomplishment thereof to establish the legal ground for God's covenanted bestowal of the eternal kingdom of salvation on his people. It was therefore expedient, if not necessary, that Christ appear within a covenant order which, like the covenant with the first Adam, was governed by the works principle (cf. Gal 4:4). The typal kingdom of the old covenant was precisely that. Within the limitations of the fallen world and with modifications peculiar to the redemptive process, the old theocratic kingdom was a reproduction of the original covenantal order. Israel as the theocratic nation was mankind stationed once again in a paradise-sanctuary, under probation in a covenant of works. In the context of that situation, the Incarnation event was legible.[33]

---

[33] Kline, *Kingdom Prologue* (Overland Park: Two Age Press, 2000), p. 352. Hereafter cited as *KP*.

The issue is redemptive-historical legibility. The incarnation and the cross of Christ have meaning only in the context of a covenantal order in which the probationary works principle is clearly in force. Imagine how inscrutable the incarnation and death of Christ would have been apart from the covenantal context provided by the Mosaic Law. It would have been an isolated "brute fact" without rhyme or reason. But the Mosaic Law republished on a grand scale the principle of works imbedded in the Adamic covenant. Israel's obedience to the Torah was the condition of her retention of the earthly kingdom, which was a type of the everlasting kingdom of heaven. Only within this legal framework do we understand "the significance of [Christ's] mission as the accomplishing of a probationary assignment in a works covenant in behalf of the elect of all ages."

Kline charges theonomy with "a misreading of the Bible on a massive scale," since it fails to "recognize that the socio-geopolitical sector of the Israelite kingdom of God was a part of the total system of kingdom typology established through the covenantal constitution given to Israel in the law of Moses -- just as much so as was the cultic sector."[34]

The cultic sector of the Mosaic Law are those laws pertaining to the restoration of sinners through a complex ritual system involving blood sacrifice. Theonomy recognizes that the cultic sector is exclusively typological. To re-enact the cultic legislation today by requiring sacrifices would be to deny that Jesus Christ is the final atonement for sin, whose sacrificial death brought the entire cultic system to its crowning conclusion. It is a redemptive historical fulfillment that does not reinforce the cultic law but terminates it.

Kline's point is that the same typological principle applies to the political sector of the Mosaic Law -- the judicial laws defining sins meriting the execution of justice by the theocratic officers of the nation. Just as the cultic sector is fulfilled by Christ's work as the

---

[34] Kline, "Comments," p. 175.

final high priest, so the political sector is fulfilled by Christ's work as the son of David, Israel's long-awaited anointed King. This fact is not based on a subtle or profound reading of the OT but something "big and plain and simple." Scripture tells us that the establishment of the Israelite kingdom was a result of the redemptive deliverance of Israel from Egypt. The Bible portrays the "Israelite king and kingdom as a redemptive, theocratic prototype of Christ and his redemptive kingdom."[35]

The Mosaic Law, then, was not given to provide a blueprint for all the civil governments of the world, but to provide the historical, covenantal context for the incarnation of Christ who was "born under the Law" in order to bring it to its perfect fulfillment (Matt. 5:17). As Paul says, Christ is "the *telos* [goal, fulfillment, terminus, completion] of the Law" (Rom. 10:4). If Paul is correct about the exclusively redemptive historical purpose of the Law as teleologically terminating in Christ, and if "the Law is good if one uses it lawfully" (1 Tim. 1:8), then Bahnsen's claim that "civil magistrates in all ages and places" are obligated to enforce the terms of the Mosaic Law is an unlawful use of the Law.[36]

(2) A biblical theological definition of theocracy

Kline's second argument against the attempt to erect Christian theocracies is that this self-assumed project involves an unbiblical notion of God's theocratic Kingdom. Kline argues that, according to the teaching of Scripture, God's theocratic Kingdom can never be equated with the kingdoms of man. God's theocratic kingdom is a unique institution established by God himself, thus relegating all pretended "theocracies" erected by men to be false imitations of God's holy kingdom.

---

[35] Kline, "Comments," p. 175.
[36] *GAP*, p. 24 (quoted above).

The peculiar kind of kingdom established in Eden at the beginning (and later redemptively renewed) differs radically from other kinds of world kingdoms that arose after the Fall. Whatever analogies exist between the theocracy and the other kingdoms, however many falsely proclaimed theocracies there may be, there is only one genuine theocratic kingdom under the special rule of the living God.[37]

Theocracy is the kingdom of God -- not merely in the general sense of God's providential reign over all of history, nor in the sense of a spiritual reign of God in the hearts of his people. Kline distinguishes between the kingdom of God *as reign* and *as realm* and argues that "though everything is embraced under the *reign* of God, not everything can be identified as part of the kingdom of God viewed as a holy *realm*."[38] Theocracy, then, is not simply God's reign, but God's reign coming to expression in a holy realm. Theocracy exists in a visible, concrete form, having clearly identifiable geopolitical boundaries. In other words, theocracy presupposes a special land that God the King claims in a special way as his own by "setting up his royal residence in the midst of the theocratic land."[39]

Another distinguishing characteristic that sets a theocratic kingdom apart from God's general providence is the "institutional coalescence of the cultic and the political" aspects. Kline calls this "the theocratic principle."[40] This can be seen most clearly in the person of the theocratic king, who governs both the political and the cultic realms, and in whom both dimensions meet. "His palace is holy; his temple is royal. His temple and palace are one." Cult and culture[41] may be governed by different theocratic officers, who serve

---

[37] *KP*, p. 49.
[38] *KP*, p. 170.
[39] *KP*, p. 49.
[40] *KP*, p. 51.
[41] *Cult* is the priestly activity of worship. In Israel, cult was formally institutionalized in the Levitical ordinances of worship that were observed daily in

under the direction of God -- i.e., priests who govern the temple and direct its cultic functions, and kings who serve as human representatives of God's royal authority.

> However, these distinguishable human functions, no matter how formally organized, would not become separated into discrete institutions (like the church and state) but would remain institutionally integrated as two functional components of the one holy institution of the theocracy. Theocracy is not a combination of church and state institutions. It is a simple unique institution, a structure *sui generis*. It is the kingdom realm whose great king is the Lord, where all activity is performed in the name of the God-King enthroned, confessed, and worshipped in the cultic epicenter, whence theocratic holiness radiates outward, permeating all, so that the whole realm, land and people, is a sanctuary of the Creator-Lord.[42]

While it may exist in various modes throughout history (whether in the pre-fall form, or in post-fall redemptive renewals of the kingdom) -- God's theocratic kingdom can only be established by God's sovereign intervention in history, and after the fall this only occurs through the historical accomplishment of the divine work of redemption. In the time before the coming of Christ, redemption occurred historically at the exodus, leading to the creation of the nation of Israel. This was only a first-level, typical redemption, not the ultimate reality, and the Israelite political kingdom was only a prototype of the coming kingdom of the

---

one centralized tabernacle/temple where God placed his name. *Culture* is the kingly activity of exercising dominion over creation -- human civilization in its totality. Israel's kingly or cultural work was subordinate to the priestly task and was therefore consecrated as holy unto God, with the eschatological goal of filling the earth as God's theocratic kingdom.

[42] *KP*, p. 51.

Messiah. With the incarnation, death, and resurrection of Christ, we now have the second-level, anti-typical redemption -- the reality itself, to which the exodus pointed. Just as the exodus led to the historical establishment of the Israelite theocratic kingdom, so the Christ-event has resulted in the inauguration of the eschatological kingdom of Christ. This was the kingdom that Jesus announced, "Repent, for the kingdom of heaven is at hand." He was not announcing the political deliverance of Israel from the Roman occupation, but the eschatological deliverance of the new Israel from the dominion of sin and death.

But what has happened to the geopolitical dimension of the kingdom as "holy realm"? The kingdom heralded and inaugurated by Christ is a theocracy, but one that unfolds in a two-stage pattern. As a semi-eschatological theocracy, the church's theocratic dimension is bound up with the mystery of the "already" and "not-yet" character of the reign of her exalted theocratic King. Presently, the church is seated with Christ in the heavenly places, reigning with him as a kingdom of priests. The earthly, visible manifestation of Christ's theocratic reign (and the church's participation therein) awaits future consummation at his second coming. The earthly, geopolitical dimension of the kingdom awaits the day when the King of kings, the ruler of the kings of the earth, returns in visible glory and power to rule the nations with a rod of iron.

This means that in the interim, while we wait for the coming of Christ in glory and judgment, the church is not to seek an earthly, political expression of Christ's present theocratic reign. According to the apostle Paul, "our citizenship is in heaven" (Phil. 3:20). As the author of Hebrews says, "We have not here an abiding city, but we seek after that which is to come" (Heb 13:14). All earthly cities -- Babylon, Rome, the United States -- shall be shaken (Heb 12:27; Ezek 38:20). As Clowney points out, the author of Hebrews is not only reminding us that the cities of this present age are passing, but he wants to drive home "the truth that Christians are not given one."[43] We are called to go with Christ outside the city, bearing his reproach (Heb 13:12-13).

On this biblical-theological understanding of the theocratic kingdom, we are enabled to address the crucial question concerning the relationship of the church to the kingdom of God. All Reformed theocrats agree that the kingdom of God is broader than the church, that the church is but one institutional form of the kingdom of God, and that other institutions (including the state) may and ought to be additional institutional expressions of God's sovereign reign in history. A biblical theological approach demands that in the present age, between the first and second comings of Christ, the one and only institutional form of the kingdom of God on earth is the non-coercive, voluntary assembly of believers fashioned into the organic, spiritual body of Christ.

Clowney argues that the church is the only sphere that can be regarded as an institutional expression of the kingdom of God prior to the return of Christ, because only "the church has the spiritual and eschatological form that the kingdom demands." One must make a clear-cut "distinction between the state as the form of the city of this world and the church as the form of the heavenly city.... Since the church anticipates the form of the world to come, it transcends the social and political forms of this world."[44] The much-maligned equation "kingdom = church" turns out actually to be valid in this particular epoch of redemptive history.

> The world cannot be sacralized ... to form the community of love Christ came to establish. The world lacks the new life of the Spirit who sheds abroad the love of Christ in human hearts. It cannot be governed by the spiritual structure of Christ's kingdom. It is the church that possesses the Spirit, and indeed is possessed by the Spirit to manifest on

---

[43] Edmund P. Clowney, "The Politics of the Kingdom," *WTJ* 41 (Spring 1979) 291-310, quote from p. 303.
[44] Clowney, pp. 306f.

earth now the realities of heaven and the age to come.[45]

In the final analysis, all attempted Christian theocracies, past and future, are doomed to fail because the state is simply not capable of being Christianized. It is too frail a vehicle for the heavenly powers of the age to come that have been set in motion through the cross and resurrection of the Son of God.

The second argument against the Reformed theocrats is that their vision of a Christian theocratic state would not qualify as a true theocracy in the first place, since the theocratic kingdom of God always comes by God's sovereign work of redemption in history, and always involves a holy realm set apart by the dwelling of God in the midst of the land. Furthermore, the notion that Christ's kingdom must achieve societal/political expression prior to the second coming of Christ involves a massive failure to do justice to the semi-eschatological, two-phase deployment of Christ's theocratic kingdom.

(3) A biblical theological definition of the state

Totally distinct from the theocratic kingdom is another biblical theological concept, also revealed in Scripture, namely, the common grace state ordained by God for man's civil government.

Kline appeals to the account of "the mark of Cain" recorded in Genesis 4 as the revealed record of God's provision of the common grace city-state.[46] After murdering his brother Abel, we are told that the LORD confronted Cain and issued the following edict, in effect a judicial pronouncement of guilt with the accompanying penalty:

---

[45] Clowney, p. 309.

[46] Kline, "Oracular Origin of the State," in *Biblical and Near Eastern Studies: Essays in Honor of William Sanford LaSor*, ed. Gary A. Tuttle (Grand Rapids: Eerdmans, 1978), pp. 132-141..

"What have you done? The voice of your brother's blood is crying to Me from the ground. Now you are cursed from the ground, which has opened its mouth to receive your brother's blood from your hand. When you cultivate the ground, it will no longer yield its strength to you; you will be a vagrant and a wanderer on the earth" (Gen. 4:10-12).

In reply, Cain expresses his fear that banishment from the protection of society is too great a punishment, for left unprotected he will be left exposed to unrestrained and capricious vigilante justice:

Cain said to the LORD, "My punishment is too great to bear! Behold, You have driven me this day from the face of the ground; and from Your face I will be hidden, and I will be a vagrant and a wanderer on the earth, and whoever finds me will kill me" (vv. 13-14).

The divine response to Cain's complaint is full of significance for the biblical theology of civil government.

So the LORD said to him, "Therefore whoever kills Cain, vengeance will be taken on him sevenfold." And the LORD appointed a sign for Cain, so that no one finding him would slay him. Then Cain went out from the presence of the LORD, and settled in the land of Nod, east of Eden (vv. 15-16).

God corrects Cain's false assumption that he was being driven into a situation of lawless vengeance. Kline argues that the statement in verse 15 that God "set a mark on Cain" is best translated, God "appointed a sign for Cain." Kline sees this not as a physical mark but as a "divine oath of judicial oversight." This opens up the possibility that God's promised protection was not intended for Cain alone, and was thus tantamount to the establishment of a system of civil justice. Why should Cain have been singled out for civil protection from lawless vigilantism? The protection given to Cain would certainly have been needed by his family as well. Accordingly, the afforded to Cain extends not only to him individually but as a public person, the head of the ungodly line.

In fact, there is evidence in the context that all men are embraced in the oracle of Genesis 4:15. In the narrative immediately following, Cain is exiled from the presence of God but he is not "a restless wanderer on the earth" (verse 12). He builds a city, the city of man (verses 16-17). Thus, the oracular oath of divine vengeance establishes a legitimate common grace order in which Cain can freely live, propagate, and build a culture in spite of his criminal past. Though he justly deserves the punishment of exile into the lawless hands of vengeance-seeking men, God graciously provides the Cainite civilization a legitimacy sanctioned by his own authority and judicial protection. Lamech's boast to his wives picks up on the tradition about the divine avenging of Cain: "I have killed a man for wounding me, and a boy for striking me. If Cain is avenged sevenfold, then Lamech seventy-sevenfold" (verses 23-24). This implies a dynastic succession of the city of man, begun by Cain and continued through the generations. Genesis 4:15, therefore "contemplates the establishment of an institutional structure for a legitimate judicial office in man's fallen world."

After the flood, the civil authority originally established among the Cainite civilization was reinstituted along with the formal enactment of the covenant of common grace:

> **Genesis 9:5-6** Surely I will require your lifeblood; from every beast I will require it. And from every man, from every man's brother I will require the life of man. Whoever sheds man's blood, by man his blood shall be shed, for in the image of God he made man.

Kline offers an insightful exegetical observation. The clause, "for in the image of God he made man" does not explain why murderers must not go unpunished, but why man is being entrusted with the God-like function of exercising judicial authority over his fellow man. This fits in with the judicial aspect of the image of God as recorded in Genesis 1:26, where the man is said to be like God because he is being entrusted with lordship and dominion over creation.

Note as well, that this civil government, initially established in Genesis 4 and reestablished after the flood in Genesis 9 is not theocratic. This is evident from the context of Genesis 9, which recounts the establishment of the covenant of common grace that God makes with "every creature" on the earth. God does not entrust the judicial task of administering justice to the covenant people of God, but to mankind in general, since man is made in God's image, irrespective of his religious confession or lack thereof. Civil government is given for the benefit of all mankind, inclusive of both the elect and the reprobate. Further supporting the non-theocratic nature of the civil institution in Genesis 9:5-6 is the fact that God ascribes no cultic functions to this institution.

In sum, civil government is not holy, nor should it be identified with God's holy kingdom of salvation. Civil government offers only temporal "salvation" in the sense of certain physical and legal protections, but by its very nature it cannot grant eternal salvation. In his common grace benevolence, God gave the good gift of civil government so that man's social life might be regulated by a civil order, and not be "abandoned to chaotic lawlessness."[47]

Having established the distinction between God's holy theocratic kingdom and the common grace institution of civil government, Kline then draws the logical conclusion that there is a "cultic boundary" separating the two spheres that may not be violated.[48] The cultic boundary may be defined as follows. Any and all cultic activity -- e.g., religious instruction, public confessions

---

[47] *KP*, pp. 163f.
[48] *KP*, p. 179.

of faith in God or any alleged pagan deity, cultic rituals such as sacrifice, the building of temples for the gods -- has no place in the common grace state. The state was ordained and established by God, and he designed that institution not in order to establish a theocratic kingdom (a task that he reserves for himself and which he alone executes by sovereign interventions in history) but in order to provide for a pragmatic cooperation between believers and unbelievers for the achievement of certain temporal ends such as physical safety, rule of law, criminal justice, and self-defense. In order to fulfill these common purposes, the state must be religiously neutral; that is, confessing allegiance neither to the God of the covenant people nor to the gods of the unbelievers.

> Every form of state participation in religious confession, whether through constitutional affirmation, official pronouncement, public ceremony, or the like, is a transgression of the boundaries set in the divine ordering of the distribution of cultural and cultic functions among the institutions of the postlapsarian world. Such cultic activity on the part of the state, if it is not in confession of the living God, is, of course, idolatrous. But even if it is in acknowledgment of the God of the Christian faith, it is guilty of a monstrous confusion of the holy kingdom of God with the common, profane city of man.[49]

Respect for the cultic boundary would entail major changes in the policy goals of many on the religious right; e.g., abandoning legislative attempts to restore school prayer. It would demand that the church adopt a civil libertarian position calling for the removal of civil confessions of faith in the public arena; e.g., "in God we trust," "God bless America," "one nation under God," and the public posting of the ten commandments. It would also mean that in policy

---

[49] *KP*, p. 180.

debates on subjects like abortion and same-sex unions, Christians must abandon appeals to Scripture and employ publicly accessible arguments grounded in religiously neutral, secular objectives.[50]

The church must resist the impulse to have the ethical standards of God's covenantal revelation in Scripture legislatively enforced in the civil sphere. Only when the church honors the cultic boundary between the common grace institution of the state and the holy kingdom of God, does the church truly honor the Lordship of Jesus Christ, for as Lord over all creation, including the civil sphere, he himself is the one who has ordained that cultic boundary (Matt. 22:21; John 18:36). What God has separated, let not man join together.

(4) Premature eclipse of common grace

Kline's final argument is that theocratic conceptions of the state are unbiblical because they necessarily involve a premature eclipse of common grace. Because it holds that the OT prophecies describing the visible, earthly kingdom of the Messiah are to be fulfilled prior to the second coming, theonomic postmillennialism postulates the premature abrogation of the common grace order. In the golden age, nations not subject to the Christocracy would be prematurely deprived of the divinely covenanted blessings of common grace.[51] On the other hand, if a state does submit to the reign of Christ, "that

---

[50] One obvious secular objective that should be a starting point for discussion is the protection of the civil liberties/rights of all citizens -- both the born and the unborn, irrespective of sexual orientation, religious allegiance, and ethnic or racial origin. To see how the political principles espoused in this essay might be applied with regard to the debate over homosexuality, see Misty Irons, "A Conservative Christian Case for Civil Same-Sex Marriage" (www.upper-register.com/theonomy/civil_same_sex_marriage.html).

[51] See, e.g., the postmillennial interpretation of a passage like Zechariah 14:16-19. The common grace blessings of rain (and thus of the provision of crops and food for the populace) would be held in abeyance as divine judgment against those nations that refuse to pay cultic homage God (as symbolically depicted in going up to the annual Feast of Booths).

too would mark the end of the institution of the common state and with it of the common grace order.... Chalcedon's postmillennialism in effect attributes unfaithfulness to God, for God committed himself in his ancient covenant to maintain that order as long as the earth endures" (Gen 8:22).[52]

Kline's argument may be set forth logically in the form of two premises and a conclusion.

Premise 1: In accordance with the covenant of common grace established after the flood, punishment of idolatry and unbelief has been suspended until the day of judgment.

There are two parts to this premise. First, the fact that God has established a covenant of common grace with mankind:

> **Genesis 8:22; 9:8-17** While the earth remains, Seedtime and harvest, and cold and heat, and summer and winter, and day and night shall not cease.... 9:8 Then God spoke to Noah and to his sons with him, saying, 9 Now behold, I Myself do establish My covenant with you, and with your descendants after you; 10 and with every living creature that is with you, the birds, the cattle, and every beast of the earth with you; of all that comes out of the ark, even every beast of the earth. 11 I establish My covenant with you; and *all flesh shall never again be cut off by the water of the flood, neither shall there again be a flood to destroy the earth....* 14 It shall come about, when I bring a cloud over the earth, that the bow will be seen in the cloud, 15 and I will remember My covenant, which is between Me and you and every living creature of all flesh; and *never again shall the water become a flood to destroy all flesh.*

---

[52] Kline, "Comments," p. 184.

The second part is that the divine punishment of unbelief and idolatry has been suspended until the day of judgment:

> **Romans 2:4** Or do you think lightly of the riches of His kindness and tolerance and patience, not knowing that the kindness of God leads you to repentance? 5 But because of your stubbornness and unrepentant heart you are storing up wrath for yourself in the day of wrath and revelation of the righteous judgment of God, 6 who will render to each person according to his deeds.

> **Romans 9:22**   What if God, although willing to demonstrate His wrath and to make His power known, endured with much patience vessels of wrath prepared for destruction?

> **2 Thessalonians 1:7-8**   ...and to give relief to you who are afflicted and to us as well when the Lord Jesus will be revealed from heaven with His mighty angels in flaming fire, dealing out retribution to those who do not know God and to those who do not obey the gospel of our Lord Jesus.

Premise 2:   In accordance with the principle of common grace, during this present time of the delay of judgment, God's present attitude toward the unbeliever is one of longsuffering patience, as evidenced in the free offer of the gospel.

> **John 3:16-17** For God so loved the world, that He gave His only begotten Son, that whoever believes in Him shall not perish, but have eternal life. For God did not send the Son into the world to judge the world, but that the world might be saved through Him.

2 Corinthians 5:18-20 Now all these things are from God, who reconciled us to Himself through Christ and gave us the ministry of reconciliation, 19 namely, that God was in Christ reconciling the world to Himself, not counting their trespasses against them, and He has committed to us the word of reconciliation. 20 Therefore, we are ambassadors for Christ, as though God were making an appeal through us; we beg you on behalf of Christ, be reconciled to God.

1 Timothy 2:3-6 This is good and acceptable in the sight of God our Savior, 4 who desires all men to be saved and to come to the knowledge of the truth. 5 For there is one God, and one mediator also between God and men, the man Christ Jesus, 6 who gave Himself as a ransom for all, the testimony given at the proper time.

2 Peter 3:9 The Lord is not slow about His promise, as some count slowness, but is patient toward you, not wishing for any to perish but for all to come to repentance.

Kline points out that the longsuffering patience and kindness of God toward unbelievers sets the pattern to be imitated by the believer. This is precisely what Jesus taught his disciples:

Matthew 5:43-45 You have heard that it was said, "You shall love your neighbor and hate your enemy." 44 But I say to you, love your enemies and pray for those who persecute you, 45 so that you may be sons of your Father who is in heaven; for He causes His sun to rise on the evil and the good, and sends rain on the righteous and the unrighteous.

Kline comments:

> The believer's attitudes toward the unbeliever are
> conditioned by the principles of common grace.
> During the historical process of differentiation which
> common grace makes possible ... the servants of
> Christ are bound by his charge to pray for the good of
> those who despitefully use and persecute them. Our
> Lord rebuked the Boanerges when they contemplated
> consuming the Samaritans with fire from heaven
> (Luke 9:54; cf. Mark 3:17). We may not seek to
> destroy those for whom, perchance, Christ has died.[53]

*Conclusion: The enforcement of the true religion by the civil
magistrate would involve a premature eclipse of the order of
common grace and would contradict the free offer of the gospel as
expressed in the church's great commission of proclaiming God's
love to a lost and dying world.*

The establishment of a Christian theocracy in the church age
is incompatible with the free offer of the gospel as committed to the
church by Jesus in the great commission. For if the civil magistrate
has a mandate from God to enforce the Christian religion, namely, to
be the agent of the execution of God's wrath against unbelief and
idolatry – then God has given contradictory commissions to these
two institutions of church and state. To the church he has entrusted
the task of being his ambassador to the world, offering to all men the
message of free amnesty from the risen King: "If you turn now and
repent, you shall be saved!" Meanwhile, to the state he has
entrusted the task of destroying those very unbelievers who are the
current recipients of the King's offer of amnesty. As Kline says, "It
is the dilemma of what would be a contradiction within God's

---

[53] Kline, *The Structure of Biblical Authority* (Eugene: Wipf and Stock, 1989), p.
161.

preceptive will, a head-on conflict between two of God's major mandates."

Reformed theocrats demand that their religious values and worldview find visible and legislative expression in the public arena. But the religious values for which they seek civil expression are grounded in the moral demands of the Law rather than in the free offer of the gospel.[54] Since the gospel calls men to living and personal faith in Jesus Christ, the gospel simply cannot be translated into a civil form without inevitably distorting it into a set of moral demands. The instrument by which all civil authority is exercised is the instrument of law and civil sanctions (enforcement). The spiritual nature of God's kingdom -- established by a mighty act of historical redemption in the Christ-event with individuals brought under the sway of the kingdom through the secret operation of the Spirit by means of the preaching the gospel and the means of grace -- is logically inconsistent with civil coercion. To wish to have the gospel of the kingdom expressed in coercive, civil form is necessarily to transform the church's great commission of bringing the good news of God's love for sinners into a theocratic conquest aimed at exterminating those very sinners whom Christ came to seek and to save.

Fully Involved Detachment

How should we then live? Should we spend all our time, money, and energy exclusively on this great commission, and thus ignore all political and cultural engagement as a waste of time? The answer is No. To properly appreciate this answer, however, we need to examine the eschatology of the New Testament. In a key ethical-eschatological text, Paul writes:

---

[54] Notice that the hot-button issues that preoccupy the political activism of the religious right in the United States tend to be matters of morality -- abortion, homosexuality, pornography, family values, etc.

1 Corinthians 7:29-31 But this I say, brethren, the time has been shortened, so that from now on those who have wives should be as though they had none; 30 and those who weep, as though they did not weep; and those who rejoice, as though they did not rejoice; and those who buy, as though they did not possess; 31 and *those who use the world, as though they did not make full use of it; for the form of this world is passing away.*

Richard Gaffin describes this attitude as one of "fully involved detachment."[55] Gaffin argues that this basic attitude flows from one's conception of New Testament eschatology. The first coming of Christ was the inbreaking of the eschatological age to come into the midst of history, while the second coming will be the final consummation of that which was set in motion by Christ's death and exaltation. This inbreaking of the future into the present relativizes the significance of the present age.[56] Marriage, earthly happiness and sorrow, material possessions -- these things belong to the present age that is "already on its way out."[57]

But Paul does not draw the ascetic conclusion that Christians should never marry or enjoy material possessions. Instead he calls for a total reorientation of our attitude in light of the age to come that has been inaugurated in Christ. Oscar Cullmann captures the nuance of Paul's position:

---

[55] Richard B. Gaffin, Jr., "Theonomy and Eschatology: Reflections on Postmillennialism," in *Theonomy: A Reformed Critique*, eds. William S. Barker and W. Robert Godfrey (Grand Rapids: Zondervan, 1990), pp.197-224..

[56] For more on the already/not-yet structure of NT eschatology, see Geerhardus Vos, *The Pauline Eschatology* (Phillipsburg: Presbyterian and Reformed Publishing Company, 1991); Herman Ridderbos, *Paul: An Outline of His Theology* (Grand Rapids: Eerdmans, 1975); Richard B. Gaffin, Jr., *Resurrection and Redemption: A Study in Paul's Soteriology* (Phillipsburg: Presbyterian and Reformed Publishing Company, 1987); Andrew T. Lincoln, *Paradise Now and Not Yet* (Grand Rapids: Baker, 1991).

[57] Gordon Fee, *The First Epistle to the Corinthians*, NICNT (Grand Rapids: Eerdmans, 1987), p. 342.

Even in the passage that seems most strongly to justify the assertion of world denial, I Cor. 7:29ff, we must hear not only the negative conclusion: "As though they made no use of the things of the world," "as though they had no wife," "as though they wept not," "as though they did not rejoice," "as though they possessed not," but we must also hear the compelling reference to the fact that they nevertheless use the things of the world, nevertheless have a wife, nevertheless weep, nevertheless rejoice, nevertheless buy.... The believer lives in a world concerning which he knows that it will pass away, but he knows that it still has its divinely willed place in the framework of redemptive history and is ruled by Christ. In so far as he knows that it will pass away, he denies it; in so far as he knows that it is the divinely willed framework of the present stage of redemptive history, he affirms it.... Simple world denial is not possible, but world affirmation is also limited ... [since the believer knows that] the form of this world passes away.[58]

Not only has the present age been dealt a decisive death blow upon the cross, after the fall there is no possibility anyway that man could ever fulfill the creation mandate in a global or eschatological sense. The creation mandate is achieved only by Christ, the second Adam, through his active and passive obedience, and through the exercise of his kingly power at his coming, when he destroys all of his and our enemies, and ushers in the new heavens and new earth. Thus, none of our cultural endeavors in the present age prior to the appearing of the second Adam will enter into the eternal city which

---

[58] Oscar Cullmann, *Christ and Time* (Philadelphia: The Westminster Press, 1950), pp. 212f.

comes down "from heaven" as a divine gift totally of God, not of man.

> The blessings of common grace endure only to the close of history. At Christ's return, pre-Consummation culture will have served its historical function and will no longer be relevant to the new order. It will be replaced by the introduction of a new Glorification-culture, the New Heavens and New Earth, produced by the supernatural intervention of God. No human labor, redeemed or unredeemed, is capable of contributing to the realization of this climactic event of redemptive history.[59]

With this eschatological perspective, there is an inevitable "detachment" in the Christian's attitude toward the common grace culture of this present age. Yet, the present age along with its common grace culture, though terminal, is the arena in which believers bear witness to the age to come as they actively engage in the daily realities of life in this world. It is not a waste of time for Christians to be engaged in the cultural, social, and political dimensions of human existence here and now. Indeed, the Christian must not separate himself from cultural activity as if it were sinful in itself, or utterly insignificant. Along with his or her attitude of eschatological detachment, the Christian ought to be "fully involved" in at least three ways.

First, the Christian must do everything to the glory of God in light of his or her union with Christ. It is incumbent upon the Christian to use his unique gifts to make a difference in whatever sphere of labor Christ has put him -- and that, for many Christians, includes politics. Paul exhorts the slaves at Ephesus to serve their masters as if they were serving Christ himself (Eph. 6:5-8). Cultural

---

[59] Mark W. Karlberg, "Covenant and Common Grace," in *Covenant Theology in Reformed Perspective* (Eugene: Wipf and Stock, 2000), pp. 297-307. This essay is an incisive review of Gary North's *Dominion and Common Grace: The Biblical Basis of Progress* (Arlington Heights: Christian Liberty Press, 1987).

common grace activity like political engagement is therefore "consecrated" to God by an internal act of faith.   It is not consecrated objectively in the sense that the activity itself will survive the fiery ordeal of judgment. Yet this internal consecration -- the attitude of our heart, by which we engage in it as unto Christ -- is not without eternal significance.   For Christ will reward his servants for all that they have done in his name. The reward will not be a meritorious quid-pro-quo but an acknowledgment from Christ that we are his faithful servants. Thus, although our cultural activity will not obtain eschatological consummation, it does possess eschatological significance.

Second, believers should cooperate with unbelievers to work for the improvement of people's lives in the present age. Involvement in the political arena is valid, not because we seek to transform the city of man into the city of God, but as a form of service to our fellow man in this life. We aren't bringing in the kingdom, but we are helping the city of man to get along better in different aspects of its social, economic, political, and cultural ordering.

Appealing to the non-theocratic politics of the patriarchs as they dwelled in the land of promise as a paradigm, Kline calls such political cooperation with unbelievers "pilgrim politics." Abraham, Isaac, and Jacob were given the promise that their seed would one day possess the land in theocratic glory. But until the day when God intervened by sovereign intervention to set up his kingdom by means of the exodus under Moses and the conquest under Joshua, the patriarchal family lived in the land as "sojourners" (Gen. 21:23, 34; 23:4; 26:3; 35:27; 47:9).[60] They were resident aliens, beholding the kingdom from a distance, and confessing that they were but strangers and exiles upon the earth (Hebrews 11:8-10, 13-16). Thus,

---

[60] A "*ger* is a man who, either alone or with his family, leaves his village and tribe, because of war, famine, pestilence, blood-guilt, etc., and seeks shelter and sojourn elsewhere, where his right to own land, to marry, and to participate in the administration of justice, in the cult, and in war is curtailed."   William L. Holladay, *A Concise Hebrew and Aramaic Lexicon of the Old Testament* (Grand Rapids: Eerdmans, 1991), p. 64.

Abraham did not take the land by force, "not even a foot of ground" (Acts 7:5), but paid Ephron the Hittite for the burial plot of Machpelah (Gen. 23).   Unlike the later theocratic command prohibiting Israel from making covenants with foreign nations (Exod. 23:32), according to the principles of pilgrim politics the patriarchs did enter into alliances with the inhabitants of the land.[61]

> Theirs was a time for the cultivation of common grace relationships, a time for toleration and cooperation with the occupants of the land.... Tolerated pilgrims, not triumphant possessors -- such is the life of the nontheocratic community of faith, waiting while the kingdom is withheld.... It is not for them, impatient with the unrealized eschatology of their day, to attempt to force the birth of the theocratic kingdom prematurely.   Perseverance in faith and patience in tribulation -- such graces become the sojourning servants of the Lord in an age of pilgrim politics.[62]

This means that we must cooperate with our fellow citizens in the earthly city -- consciously including those who are not members of the holy kingdom of God by saving union with Christ -- for the purpose of making the city of man a more habitable place for all its citizens.   Our goals are purely temporal, and pertain only to the interim order of common grace established by God for the benefit of all mankind during the time of the delay of eschatological judgment.   The political activities of Christians must not appear to be self-serving, seeking the legislative implementation of our own

---

[61] See Abraham's and Isaac's covenants with the Philistine king Abimelech for the purpose of settling disputes over wells (Gen. 21:22-32; 26:12-33). Also, Genesis 14:13 mentions three Amorite brothers (Mamre, Eschol, and Aner) who were "allies [lit. masters of a covenant] with Abram." This federation obviously included promises of mutual defense, as can be seen in the subsequent story of their successful military campaign against Chedorlaomer and his alliance of kings.

[62] *KP*, pp. 356-60.

religious ideals upon an unwilling, pluralistic populace. Instead, all that we do must be service-oriented, as we seek like good Samaritans to bind up the wounds of our fellow man, showing neighborly concern for his temporal welfare. We have no illusions of grandeur as we go about seeking such temporal goods. We know that Ecclesiastes is ultimately right, that, this side of heaven, all of our work is striving after wind, since it is plagued by sin, by the ravages of the fall and the curse, and by our own shortcomings. Common grace work can't remove the effects of the curse. It can't provide ultimate happiness -- contrary to the utopian ideals of many secularists on the left. The ideal form of civil existence, free of all suffering, discord, and unhappiness, must wait until the coming of our Savior in glory at the end of time. But while we wait, we must serve Christ by serving our fellow man and bearing witness to a greater and more lasting hope in heaven.

Third, cultural and political engagement on the part of Christians is valuable as part of our witness to the world. Insofar as people see us doing these things for the good of our fellow man, constrained by the love of Christ, these become good works that cause men to glorify our Father in heaven. They observe that we are seeking to serve others rather than looking for triumphalistic victory. Unbelievers take note that, unlike the utopians of the left, we are prepared for a mixture of failures and successes. When unbelievers see that we are not totally despondent when we encounter disappointment and difficulty, we explain the reason: we have a better hope in heaven. When they see that we are not elated by (momentary) success, again it is because we have a better hope in heaven. Although we may use such service as an opportunity to bring to our neighbor the good news of eternal welfare available only in Christ the Savior, such witness bearing is ancillary and does not sacralize the concrete policy goals that we pursue in cooperation with the unbeliever.

In all of this, our ultimate priority will remain the work of the Kingdom of Jesus Christ by means of the preaching of the gospel and the building up of the church. The kingdom does not advance through political means, but through the preaching of Christ and him crucified.

> The saving rule of God's kingdom spreads among the nations through his weak but faithful servants, who proclaim the folly of the cross in the hidden power of the Spirit. And it calls us, even as we pursue evangelism and justice in the present age, to look ahead to the only perfect disclosure of the kingdom's righteousness, at the coming of the King, Jesus Christ.[63]

We must be heavenly-minded, living in the conscious awareness that we are a pilgrim church on the path to a heavenly city. This does not mean we retreat from the world in pious detachment, but that we live as disciples of Jesus Christ -- living for the same purpose for which he lived and died: to seek and save the lost. Our "political agenda" is to build the New Community, the colony of heaven on earth, the church -- by evangelism, worship, Christian nurture, and ministries of mercy. Only as the church conforms to this heavenly pattern, will it be "a city set on a hill" and "the salt of the earth."[64]

Conclusion

National confessionalist William Edgar laments what he considers to be a defeatist attitude prevalent among many American Christians:

> Over the last two hundred years the church has endured so many defeats that believers no longer

---

[63] Dennis E. Johnson, "The Epistle to the Hebrews and the Mosaic Penal Sanctions," pp. 171-92 in *Theonomy: A Reformed Critique* (see footnote 55).
[64] Clowney, "The Politics of the Kingdom," p. 302.

think that it is Jesus' plan to call whole nations to be Christian. The most that American believers hope for is to convert individuals, establish Christian families, influence a few minor institutions on the fringes of society, and slow down society's moral degradation. American Christians have been so affected by defeatist theologies ... that they unthinkingly reject the possibility or desirability of a Christian nation.[65]

According to the Reformed theocrats, apparently, it is not enough to "convert individuals, establish Christian families," and (presumably) labor toward the ongoing reformation of the church. To "settle" for such non-triumphalistic goals is "defeatist." The only satisfactory goal is that America become a Christian nation. For these theocrats, the Christian church will -- by definition -- continue to endure defeat and discouragement until the day when Christian values have been adopted at the highest levels of national government. It is not sufficient that we see growth in the realms of personal and family morality and of voluntary associations of like-minded believers (i.e., the church and other institutions like private Christian schools). Why not? Because these arenas of religious expression are voluntary (as opposed to coercive), private (as opposed to public), permitted (as opposed to legislatively favored), and benevolent (as opposed to triumphalistic).

Thinking that the disestablishment of the church is the cause of its cultural ineffectiveness, Reformed fundamentalists long for a revival of Christian theocracy. But if the humble proclamation of the King's gracious amnesty is the present function of the church (and thus the present form of the kingdom of Christ prior to the second coming), then coercive, public, legislatively favored and triumphalist means of advancing Christ's kingdom must be renounced. Otherwise the church's witness to the gospel of grace and to a coming eschatological kingdom not of this world, will be transmogrified into a grotesque perversion of that gospel and of that

---

[65] *GAP*, p. 191.

kingdom. Ironically, then, it is the wholesale *rejection* (not revival) of theocratic principles that is desperately needed today if the church is to be faithful to the task of gospel witness entrusted to her in the present age. It is only as the church is conformed to her Head, the Suffering Servant, who came not to be served, but to serve and to give his life as a ransom for many -- it is only as the church learns to be satisfied with God's eschatological timetable, and thus puts aside the lust for worldly influence and power -- that she will be a positive presence in society.

J. Gresham Machen said, "Reasonable persuasion can thrive only in an atmosphere of liberty. It is quite useless to approach a man with both a club and an argument. He will very naturally be in no mood to appreciate our argument until we lay aside our club."[66] If we approach the world as homeless pilgrims rather than as club-wielding triumphalists, perhaps more "reasonable persuasion" will thrive in our culturally polarized society. Perhaps our message will not be dismissed as a merely self-serving agenda. Thus stripped down, we will only be better ambassadors for Christ, as though God himself were making his appeal through us, beseeching all men and women to be reconciled to God. "For God so loved the world, that he gave his only begotten Son, that whosoever believes in him should not perish, but have eternal life."

---

[66] Quoted by Ned B. Stonehouse, *J. Gresham Machen: A Biographical Memoir* (Edinburgh: The Banner of Truth Trust, 1987), p. 403.

Bibliography

Bahnsen, Greg L. *No Other Standard: Theonomy and Its Critics.* Tyler: Institute for Christian Economics, 1991.

----. *Theonomy in Christian Ethics.* Phillipsburg: Presbyterian and Reformed Publishing Company, 1984.

Clowney, Edmund P. "The Politics of the Kingdom." *Westminster Theological Journal* 41 (1979), pp. 291-310.

Cullmann, Oscar. *Christ and Temple.* Philadelphia: The Westminster Press, 1950.

Fee, Gordon. *The First Epistle to the Corinthians.* NICNT. Grand Rapids: Eerdmans, 1987.

Gaffin, Richard B., Jr. "Theonomy and Eschatology: Reflections on Postmillennialism." *Theonomy: A Reformed Critique.* Ed. William S. Barker and W. Robert Godfrey. Grand Rapids: Zondervan, 1990.

Goold, William H. (Ed.). *The Works of John Owen. Vol. XIII.* London & Edinburgh: Johnstone and Hunter, 1852.

Gordon, T. David. "Critique of Theonomy: A Taxonomy." *Westminster Theological Journal* 56 (1994), pp. 23-43.

Holladay, William L. *A Concise Hebrew and Aramaic Lexicon of the Old Testament.* Grand Rapids: Eerdmans, 1991.

Karlberg, Mark W. "Covenant and Common Grace." *Covenant Theology in Reformed Perspective.* Eugene: Wipf and Stock, 2000.

Kline, Meredith G. Review of *Dominion Theology: Blessing or Curse? An Analysis of Christian Reconstructionism,* by H. Wayne House and Thomas Ice in *Journal of Church and State* 31 (Autumn 1989), pp. 577-578.

----. "Comments on an Old-New Error." *Westminster Theological Journal* 41 (1978), pp. 172-189.

----. *Kingdom Prologue.* Overland Park: Two Age Press, 2000.

----. "Oracular Origin of the State." *Biblical and Near Eastern Studies: Essays in Honor of William LaSor*. Ed. Gary A. Tuttle. Grand Rapids: Eerdmans, 1978.

----. *The Structure of Biblical Authority*. Eugene: Wipf and Stock, 1989.

Marsden, George M. *The Evangelical Mind and the New School Presbyterian Experience*. New Haven: Yale University Press, 1970.

North, Gary. *Dominion and Common Grace: The Biblical Basis of Progress*. Arlington Heights: Christian Liberty Press, 1987.

North, Gary (Ed.). Theo*nomy: An Informed Response*. Tyler: Institute for Christian Economics, 1991.

Smart, Ninian. *The World's Religions*. 2nd Revised Edition. Cambridge: Cambridge University Press, 1998.

Smith, Gary Scott (Ed.). *God and Politics: Four Views on the Reformation of Civil Government*. Phillipsburg: Presbyterian and Reformed Publishing Company, 1989.

Stonehouse, Ned B. *J. Gresham Machen: A Biographical Memoir*. Edinburgh: The Banner of Truth Trust, 1987.

"In like manner, while the government of the world places the doctrine of providence beyond dispute, the practical result is the same as if it were believed that all things were carried hither and thither at the caprice of chance; so prone are we to vanity and error. I am still referring to the most distinguished of the philosophers, and not to the common herd, whose madness in profaning the truth of God exceeds all bounds."

John Calvin

The Institutes of the Christian Religion

"City of God"

David Kim

Student For Christ (SFC)
USA

Introduction

In our days, there is no dearth of discussion and debate about peace:
what it is, and how we achieve it. In search for an answer, many
have and are recently turning to one person who has struggled with
the question of peace all of his life and has made it a central theme
in his works -- Augustine of Hippo. The *locus classicus* for the
theme of peace is Book XIX of the *City of God.*[1]

---

[1] O'Daly notes that it is perhaps the most studied part of the *City of God.* Gerald
O'Daly, *Augustine's City of God: A Reader's Guide* (Oxford: Clarenden Press,
1999), 196.

What is obvious about Book XIX to most readers is, as the title of the 19.17 suggests ("What produces peace between the heavenly city and the earthly city"), that the discussion of peace in Book XIX, with its implication of the relationship between the heavenly city and the earthly city, forms the climax of the *City of God*.

However, what is not so obvious is what exactly constitutes that interaction or what produces peace between the heavenly city and the earthly city. It should be made clear at this point that Augustine is not rejecting his absolute antithesis between heavenly city and earthly city, in terms of their religious commitments. What Augustine seeks to do is to find the ways in which the heavenly city can relate to the earthly city *via* the earthly *peace*. The question that Augustine seeks to answer in 19.17 is then: How do the heavenly city and earthly city relate to the earthly peace?

The interpretation of this relationship is of utmost importance, for it is the hinge upon which much of one's interpretation of Augustinian political thought rests. The goal of this paper is to revisit the *City of God* 19.17 and compare it with the interpretations of three prominent modern and postmodern interpreters, namely Robert Markus, John Milbank, and Jean Bethke Elshtain, and to show that, though these interpreters have some insights into Augustine's understanding of peace, ultimately they do not do justice to it.

Revisiting 19.17 of *City of God*

Before we delve into the *City of God* 19.17, a quick overview of the perspectives of the three scholars in question will be helpful. First, Robert Markus' view is that the earthly peace consists of some neutral ground between the heavenly city and the earthly city. [2]

---

[2] Robert Markus, *Saeculum: History and Society in the Theology of St. Augustine* (Cambridge: Cambridge University Press, 1970), 68.

Second view is that of John Milbank, who believes that even though the heavenly city uses the earthly peace, there is an inherent problem in using earthly peace.[3] Third view is that of Jean Bethke Elshtain, who holds that heavenly peace cannot become a reality in the *earthly cities* but that *making* earthly peace is a way of participating in the heavenly peace.[4] John Milbank reacts to Robert Markus, and Jean Elshtain reacts to both Robert Markus and John Milbank. The response of John Milbank is considered "radical orthodox," that of Jean Elshtain, "postmodern," and that of Robert Markus, "modern." In short, the three scholars fall short of understanding Augustine's concept of peace in a way that keeps the balance between, on the one hand, the antithesis between the earthly peace and the heavenly peace, and on the other, the continuity between the two, as I will argue Augustine does. That is to say, Augustine neither absolutizes one at the expense of the other (as Milbank tends to do), nor relativizes them (as both Markus and Elshtain tend to do). Or yet to put it in another way, Augustine wants to maintain that there is a legitimate way of using the earthly peace, and that the role of the heavenly peace in achieving that is absolutely essential. Before we examine each of these scholars' understanding of Augustinian peace more closely and how it functions in their larger aims, we will examine the ways in which Augustine calls the heavenly city to relate to the earthly peace in 19.17 of *City of God*.

Two Ways in Which the Heavenly City is Called to Relate to the Earthly Peace

We want to begin our examination with the last paragraph of 19.17, which is essentially a summary of how the heavenly city relates to

---

[3] John Milbank, *Theology & Social Theory: Beyond Secular Reason* (Oxford: Blackwell, 1993), 407.

[4] Jean Bethke Elshtain, *Augustine and a Politics of Limits* (Notre Dame: University of Notre Dame Press, 1995), 105.

the earthly peace, pointing out the two ways in which the heavenly city is called to relate to the earthly peace.

> Even the heavenly city, therefore, while in its state of pilgrimage, **avails** itself of the peace of earth, and, so far as it can without injuring faith and godliness, desires and maintains a common agreement among men regarding the acquisition of the necessaries of life, and makes this earthly peace **bear** upon the peace of heaven; **for this** alone can be truly called and esteemed the peace of the reasonable creatures, consisting as it does in the perfectly ordered and harmonious enjoyment of God and of one another in God. When we shall have reached that peace, this mortal life shall give place to one that is eternal, and our body shall be no more this animal body which by its corruption weighs down the soul, but a spiritual body feeling no want, and in all its members subjected to the will. In its pilgrim state the heavenly city possesses **this** peace by faith; and by this faith it lives righteously when it **refers** to the attainment of **that** peace every good action towards God and man; for the life of the city is a social life.[5]

---

[5] Bold Mine. English versions usually have more relative pronouns "this" or "that," since they separate the long Latin sentence into smaller sentences, which makes it harder to locate the referents. A typical example is that of Marcus Dods in the *Post-Nicene Fathers Series*, in *The City of God* (Chicago: Encyclopaedia Britannica, Inc., 1952). The corresponding Latin for the above passage is here quoted from http://ccat.sas.upenn.edu/jod/. These texts were compiled in conjunction with the *AugustinusLexikon* project (Würzburg/Gießen, Germany by C. P. Mayer, O.S.A.):

> **utitur** ergo etiam caelestis ciuitas in hac sua peregrinatione pace terrena et de rebus ad mortalem hominum naturam pertinentibus humanarum uoluntatum conpositionem, quantum salua pietate ac religione conceditur, tuetur atque adpetit eamque ter- renam pacem **refert** ad caelestem pacem, **quae** uere ita pax est, ut rationalis dum- taxat creaturae sola pax habenda atque dicenda

The first way the heavenly city is called to relate to the earthly peace is in the context of "universal grace" (common grace),[6] which is found at least three times in chapter 17: (1) "The heavenly city . . . *avails* itself of the peace of earth, so far as it can without injuring faith and godliness, desires and maintains a common agreement among men regarding the acquisition of the necessaries of life." (2) "*use*...such advantages of time and of earth as do not fascinate and divert them from God, but rather aid them to endure with greater ease, and to keep down the number of those burdens of the corruptible body," (3) "because it must be *used*, until this mortal condition which necessitates it shall pass away." In each of these three instances, the word "use" (twice *utitur,* once *utatur*) is used and all of them are in the context of enjoying the earthly peace as a "universal peace."[7]

In contrast, in the latter part of chapter 17, we have another way in which the heavenly city is called to be related to the earthly peace -- in the context of the special grace. The contrast is signaled

---

sit, ordinatissima scilicet et concordissima societas fruendi deo et inuicem in deo; quo cum uentum erit, non erit uita mortalis, sed plane certeque uitalis nec corpus animale, quod, dum corrumpitur, adgrauat animam, sed spiritale sine ulla indigentia ex omni parte subditum uoluntati. hanc pacem, dum peregrinatur in fide, habet atque ex hac fide iuste uiuit, cum ad illam pacem adipiscendam **refert** quidquid bonarum actionum gerit erga deum et proximum, quoniam uita ciuitatis utique socialis est.

[6] Augustine's use of the phrase "universal peace" is very similar to Calvin's use of the phrase "common grace" in that the "universal peace" is clearly distinguished from "heavenly peace" (*Institutes,* 2.2.17). For example, even though in his "taxonomy of peace" in 19.13, Augustine does not seem to distinguish between "universal" and "heavenly" peace, he clearly does in 19.14. In chapter 27, he distinguishes the two with the phrases, "peace which is common to all" and "peace which is peculiar to ourselves [heavenly city in pilgrimage]."

[7] The only other time the word "use" occurs by itself (not with "refer") in relation to "peace" in Book XIX is chapter 26, where the context is also that of universal peace.

by the use of the word "refer" (*refert*). This word occurs twice in
the entire chapter, and both occur in this latter part, once where it is
translated "earthly peace *bear* upon the peace of heaven,"[8] and then
once again in the last sentence, "refers to the attainment of that
peace." This word "refer" is used in a much more active sense of
"directing," which is how some have translated the word,[9] than the
word "use." More specifically, this word is used in two different
senses.

First, it means "to have as the goal or end." This is
suggested by the phrase "refer to the *attainment*" in the last sentence
of 19.17: "In its pilgrim state the heavenly city possesses this peace
by faith; and by this faith it lives righteously when it refers to the
attainment of that peace every good action towards God and man."
In other words, every good action towards God and man has as its
goal the attainment of that [heavenly] peace.

Secondly, the word "refer" refers to the *means* of
accomplishing the earthly peace -- and this means is faith, faith in
God who grants the heavenly peace. This is suggested by the first
half of the same last sentence: "by this faith" one lives
"righteously," *when* it "refers to the attainment of that peace." Here
"lives righteously by faith" is instantiated with "referring to the
attainment of heavenly peace" so that an example of having faith is
the activity of this "referring." In other words, referring all our good
actions to the attainment of the heavenly peace requires that we have
faith, and that we already possess, in some measure, the heavenly

---

[8] Gerald G. Walsh and Daniel J. Honan's translation in *The Fathers of the Church*
series for this first use of "refert" as "subordinate" -- so that it reads "the *City of
God* subordinates this earthly peace to that of heaven" -- is very misleading. *Saint
Augustine: The City of God* (New York: Fathers of the Church, 1954), 228.
[9] "Directing" is a better translation and it is used for both occurrences by R. W.
Dyson in his translation in Augustine, The *City of God* (Cambridge: Cambridge
University Press, 1998), 947; and by Michael W. Tkacz and Douglas Kries in
Augustine, *Political Writings* (Indianapolis: Hackett Publishing Company, 1994),
158. John Healey's translation of Latin *refert* as "make use," is therefore very
misleading. John Healey, trans, *The City of God*, ed. R.V.G. Tasker (New York:
E. P. Dutton, 1962), 255.

peace. In other words, in all actions, Christians are called to seek after the heavenly peace, because it is possible, and because they have already tasted, though small it may be, the truly heavenly peace. Or simply, more true peace is available to those who have already received by faith from God.[10]

This double sense of goal and motive is also contained in the other instance of "refer" in Book XIX.

> And because, so long as he is in this mortal body, he is a stranger to God, he walks by *faith*, not by sight; and he therefore **refers** all peace, bodily or spiritual or both, to that peace which mortal man has with the immortal God, so that he exhibits the well-ordered obedience of faith to eternal law.[11]

The only other instance "refer" (*refert*) is used in the entire Book XIX is in chapter 10, and there it is used in the context of discussion of virtue, which also has the eternal peace as the goal.

The Inseparability Between the Two Ways of Relating to the Earthly Peace

In analyzing 19.17, what seems to emerge is that Augustine is rhetorically emphasizing not only the difference between the two ways in which the heavenly city is called to relate to the earthly peace, [12] but also the inseparability between the two. That is to say,

---

[10] This is a central notion in Augustinian ethics. He applies the same principle to his understanding of true love. One can love others and even themselves in a true sense only when one "refers" those loves to the love of God. Augustine, *On Christian Doctrine,* trans. D. W. Robertson, Jr. (Upper Saddle River: Prentice Hall, 1997), I.22., 19.

[11] *City of God*, 520. Bold Mine.

[12] The two words "use" and "refer" occur together in chapters 10 and 20, but it is only in chapter 17 that there is such a rhetorical effect.

Augustine seems to be emphasizing *both* the need to pursue after earthly peace in the context of common grace, as well as the need to *refer* it to the heavenly peace in the context of special grace. Furthermore, Augustine wants to emphasize the unique privilege that Christians have in being able to pursue after both. This is the radical difference between a member of the city of God and a member of the city of earth. The former can possess the heavenly peace and can pursue after earthly peace that is eternally significant. The latter can have neither. They can only possess earthly peace that is temporally significant.

The two contexts of relating to the earthly peace have great implications in Augustinian political theory. Christians, or the members of the *City of God*, are called to respond to both, and not separately, or one at the expense of another. Augustine's genius lies in holding these two contexts in tandem, so that pursuing after earthly peace is the context and referring it to the heavenly peace is the content. The context and the content need each other. On the one hand, Augustine wants to warn the Christians not to pursue earthly peace for the sake of earthly peace. He points out in chapter 26: "Yet even [the people without faith] has a peace of its own which is not to be lightly esteemed, though, indeed, it shall not in the end enjoy it, because it makes no good use of it before the end." On the other hand, Augustine is calling the Christians to engage in pursuing earthly peace in the context of heavenly peace. In the same context of chapter 26, Augustine recites both an example from the Old Testament and an example from the New Testament to support this:

> And therefore the apostles also admonished the Church to pray for kings and those in authority, assigning as the reason, "that we may live a quiet and tranquil life in all godliness and love." And the prophet Jeremiah when predicting the captivity that was to befall the ancient people of God, and giving them the divine command to go obediently to Babylonia, and thus serve their God, counseled them

also to pray for Babylonia saying, "In the peace thereof shall ye have peace."[13]

Thus, we can see from these examples that Augustine's understanding of pursuit of true peace is in pursuing after the heavenly peace in the *context* of pursuing after the earthly peace.[14] The implication of this again is that Augustine's vision of the "perfectly ordered and harmonious enjoyment of God and of one another in God" refers not merely to the heavenly city at the end of time, but also to the *City of God* in its pilgrim state, as well as the realm of the *saeculum* -- that is in all the realms in the entire temporal period between the Fall and the end-time. Again, this is suggested by the last clause of 19.17: "for the life of the city is a social life."[15] This last clause is not merely pointing to the social life of the heavenly city, but the social life in general, thereby validating the possibility of enjoying God and one another in the *saeculum* by referring them to the heavenly peace. The last paragraph from chapter 13 also supports this understanding:

> God, then, the most wise Creator and most just
> Ordainer of all natures, who placed the human race
> upon earth as its greatest ornament, imparted to men
> some good things, adapted to this life, to wit,
> *temporal peace,* such as we *can enjoy in this life from*
> *health and safety and human fellowship,* and from

---

[13] Augustine, *City of God* 19.26, trans. Marcus Dods [Nicene and Post-Nicene Fathers Series] (Chicago: Encyclopaedia Britannica, Inc., 1952), 529.

[14] This idea is further developed by Calvin in his *Institutes*, regarding the relationship between Christians and the civil government. Calvin shows clearly the different contexts of the two kingdoms (special grace in God's kingdom and common grace in civil government), as well as the connection between the two: "For spiritual government, indeed is already initiating in us upon earth certain beginnings of the Heavenly Kingdom, and in this mortal and fleeting life affords a certain forecast of an immortal and incorruptible blessedness." John Calvin, *Institutes of the Christian* Religion, ed. John T. McNeill (Philadelphia: The Westminster Press, 1960), 1485-1521.

[15] Augustine, *City of God*, 523.

things needful for the preservation and recover of this peace, such as the objects which are accommodated to our outward senses, light, night, the air, and waters suitable for us, and everything the body requires to sustain, shelter, heal, or beautify it: *and all under this most equitable condition*, that every man who made a good use of these advantages suited to the peace of this mortal condition, should receive ampler and better blessings, namely, the peace of immortality, accompanied by glory and honor in an endless life made fit for the enjoyment of God and of one another in God; but that he who used the present blessings badly should both lose them and should not receive the others.[16]

Under the condition that the temporal peace is used with the motivation and the goal of the peace of immortality in mind, temporal peace could be enjoyed in a genuinely, and even eternally meaningful way. Summing up Augustine's understanding of true peace in Book XIX of the City of God, true peace is received by faith, and practiced or applied in the context of securing earthly peace, with the goal of referring it to the heavenly peace.

An Example in Practice

This way of understanding the relationship between earthly peace and heavenly peace is not just a theory but actually promoted by Augustine in life. An example is seen in his letter to Darius, a high ranking imperial official who was a Christian and a friend of Augustine. In 427/428 Darius was dispatched to Africa from Italy

---

[16] *City of God*, 519-520. Italics Mine.

to end the fighting between Boniface and imperial troops, the effort of which was apparently successful.[17]

> There are written the words of Truth himself:
> *Blessed are the peacemakers, for they shall be called*
> *the sons of God* [Mt 5:9]. Greatness and their own
> glory belong to warriors who are both very brave and
> very faithful (that is the source of the truer praise), to
> those who struggle and face danger in order, with the
> help of God who gives protection and assistance, to
> bring defeat upon an untamed enemy and win respite
> for the empire by pacifying the provinces. However,
> greater glory still is merited by killing not men with
> swords, but war with words, and by acquiring or
> achieving peace not through war but through peace
> itself. For those who fight, if they are good men, are
> certainly aiming for peace, but still through
> bloodshed. By contrast, you were sent to avoid any
> blood being shed. For others, then, the one is a
> necessity; for you, the other is a joy…. Therefore,
> my … beloved son in Christ … rejoice that so great
> and true a good is yours and enjoy it in God, who has
> enabled you to be such a person and to undertake
> such an enterprise.[18]

We notice that Augustine begins with "blessed are the peacemakers" and includes as peacemakers both those who fight physically to bring peace, as well as Darius who was sent to bring peace through words. The difference is that whereas those who fought, did it out of "necessity" (common grace), Darius did it out of joy and God's enablement (special grace). That is not to say that others did it out of grudge, or that Darius did not do it out of necessity. The difference is between common grace and special

---

[17] Augustine, *Political Writings*, ed. E. M. Atkins and R. J. Dodaro (Cambridge: Cambridge University Press, 2001), 233

[18] Augustine, *Political Writings*, 225. Letter 229: Augustine to Darius (429/430).

grace. However, both are blessed and both are "great" because both did it to make peace, and both did it out of their commitment or faith in God. Augustine says that Darius has the greater glory for resolving war with peace, but we need to note that both the soldiers and Darius are commended for their faith, which Augustine calls "the source of the truer praise." Both are commended with Mt 5:9 verse: "Blessed are the peacemakers," soldiers in the context of war, Darius in the context of diplomacy. This extreme example of war starkly shows the two inseparable aspects in pursuing after earthly peace: (1) Christians must engage in pursuing after peace, even in the above context of a just war, and cannot exempt themselves from involving in the world, (2) Securing earthly peace, even through war, is meaningless, if it is not done in faith and commitment to God. On the one hand, Augustine avoids denying Christians' role in the public and the use of earthly peace (even via war, sometimes). On the other, he avoids any neutrality in respect to that role. We will now turn to the three scholars mentioned above to see how each of them falls short of maintaining this balance.

Robert Markus

Weakness of Markus' Interpretation

In the celebrated work *Saeculum,* Robert Markus gives his interpretation to *City of God* Book XIX. Markus interprets Augustine as having created a neutral space in the public life, a political sphere that is exclusive of one's religious values:

> The discussion of Book XIX of the *City of God* in effect pushed such fundamental commitments as a man's religious beliefs and the values he lives by outside the field of political discourse.[19]

---

[19] Markus, 70.

According to Markus' reading, Augustine severed the "realm of politics" and the "realm of faith," with the only link between the two being the inward realm of the individual.[20] Markus then spells out the implications of this idea: ". . . the functions, institutions, and the quality of a society cannot be assessed in terms of the ultimates of human destiny. . ."[21] In short, Markus attributes to Augustine the creation of *saeculum* as a "religiously neutral civil community,"[22] where people with different ultimate loyalties can work together to produce some common good or "temporal peace."

In coming to this conclusion, Markus says that Augustine was speaking of an "overlap" between the heavenly city and the earthly city.

> The existence of a wide range of activity which forms the proper object of concern to all men, whatever the values to which they are ultimately committed, accounts for the overlap of the two cities in this realm. The earthly peace is of common concern to all, whether citizens of the heavenly or of the earthly cities; it is valued and 'loved' by both." Augustine's 'positivistic' definition of the *res publica* appears to have been very carefully devised to make room for this overlap.[23]

The understanding of this "overlap," in turn is grounded upon his interpretation of Book XIX: "In Book XIX of the *City of God* he set about the task of defining a secular sphere in which it was possible for a Christian to think of himself as a member of a temporarily limited society."[24] More specifically determinative for Markus' interpretation is a sentence in 19.17, which he translates:

---

[20] Markus, 70.

[21] Markus, 104.

[22] Markus, 173.

[23] Markus, 69.

[24] Markus, 102.

"All share in 'using' these (temporal) things, but each has his own purpose in using them, and the purposes differ widely."[25] This sentence actually refers to the difference between the heavenly city and the earthly city, but Markus interprets it as also referring to the different members in the earthly city:

> The people constituting a *res publica* are agreed in valuing certain things....   So far as these are concerned, within its restricted sphere, the state is inherently "pluralistic", being the sphere in which the concerns of individuals with divergent ultimate loyalties coincide. The worlds of their personal valuations may be differently structured, their personal orientations in respect of what is ultimately desirable may conflict; but this does not preclude agreement on valuing in some manner which need not --indeed must not -- be specified, all that Augustine includes within the scope of "temporal peace."[26]

Oliver O'Donovan suggests how Markus could have misread the text. He points out that it is:

> Easiest mistake in the world for the casual reader to take the words rendered "similarly" (*ita etiam*) to refer to what has gone immediately before: the *City of God* and the earthly city get on together by having a common use and differing ends.   From this misreading we would conclude that the earthly city is a neutral institution of shared means to private ends.[27]

---

[25] *Communis est usus; sed finis utendi cuique suus proprius, multumque diversus -- City of God* 19.17. in Markus, 68.

[26] Markus, 69.

[27] Oliver O'Donovan, "Augustine's *City of God* XIX and Western Political Thought," in *The City of God: A Collection of Essays*, ed. Dorothy F. Donnelly (New York: Peter Lang, 1995), 140.

In sum, this misinterpretation led Markus to see the *saeculum* as a "religiously neutral civil community." Another main weakness of Markus' interpretation is that it is too individualistic. John Milbank is particularly critical of this: "Certain commentators, notably R. A. Markus, attempts to play down Augustine's explicit identification of the visible, institutional Church with the *"City of God* on pilgrimage through this world."[28]

Strength of Markus' Interpretation

The strength of Markus' interpretation is in that he shows the distinct contrast between believers and non-believers as individuals. For Markus, the Church and the State are realms in which different individuals may have "fundamentally differing structures of motivation."[29] The upshot of Markus' interpretation is that while there is much ambiguity on the institutional level, there is ample room for action and change on the individual level. The sphere of politics is seen as "a matter of deep concern to the citizen of the heavenly city."[30]

Another strength of Markus' interpretation is Augustine's desacralization of Christendom -- the separation of the Church with the *City of God*. The achievements of the earthly city are "radically infected with the ambiguity of all human achievement."[31]

In sum, Markus' understanding of the relationship between the heavenly peace and the earthly peace is one of a negative kind. A Christian contributes to the earthly peace by "disturbing the false peace." Furthermore, the gap between the visible, historic Christian church and the *City of God* is maximized, and therefore the link between heavenly peace and earthly peace is minimized. Rather, for

---

[28] Milbank, *Theology and Social Theory,* 402.

[29] Milbank, *Theology and Social Theory*, 70.

[30] Milbank, *Theology and Social Theory,* 71.

[31] Markus, 35, 42.

Markus, the "concern for the *saeculum* is the temporal dimension of his concern for the eternal city."[32]

John Milbank

Strength of Milbank's Interpretation

Twenty-three years after the publication of Markus' *Saeculum*, John Milbank publishes *Theology and Social Theory*, which provides a radically different and new interpretation to the relationship between the heavenly peace and earthly peace. In this book, Milbank takes a radically different view from Markus, and deconstructs the "secular." He shows that there is no such neutral ground, according to Augustine. He shows that every social theory has a theological agenda and basis. Milbank's thesis is simple: against all social theories which pretends they are neutral or which are man-centered, there is the Christian alternative with its "counter-history," "counter-ethics," and "counter-ontology." In Milbanks's view, Augustine provides the most successful Christian example of a "metanarrative realism" which can criticize both secular society and the church itself on the basis of resources provided entirely from within the Christian tradition.[33] Milbank shows that what makes Christians different from all other traditions is that it is marked by peaceful reconciliation. Milbank sees Augustine's most fundamental contribution not as the baleful effects of the original sin, as the liberals do,[34] but as the absolute priority of peace over violence and antagonism of every kind. Milbank criticizes the liberal individualist reading of Augustine as failing to recognize the degree

---

[32] Markus., 102.

[33] Milbank, *Theology and Social Theory,* 382.

[34] Michael J. Hollerich, "Milbank and Augustine" in *History, Apocalypse, and the Secular Imagination: New Essays on Augustine's City of God,* ed. Mark Vessey, Karla Pollmann, Allen D. Fitzgerald, O.S.A. (Bowling Green: Bowling Green State University, 1990), 317.

to which Augustine sees the church itself as a "political" reality that strives to embrace the whole of our social life and whose inclusivity therefore far exceeds that of the ancient *polis*.[35]

In comparison, then to Markus, Milbank's interpretation offers a much more active role of the heavenly city. While for Markus, only individuals function as "disturbers of peace," Milbank shows that the church as an institution provides an "alternative political force," as an earthly embodiment of heavenly peace.

Weakness of Milbank's Interpretation

However, while Milbank's strength is in offering an active role of the heavenly peace as embodied by the church, his weakness is in overemphasizing the communal nature of peace, at the expense of the role of the individual. He says that "salvation is only in common: it is only the peace of the *altera civitas*."[36] Even in the relationship between the heavenly peace and the earthly peace, Milbank is forced to conclude that the action of an individual is valid only to the extent that he subordinates it under ecclesial purpose: "the Christian ruler will make *usus* of the earthly peace, by subordinating it to the ecclesial purposes of charity . . ."[37]

This emphasis on the communal nature of peace and the close identification of the visible Church with the *City of God* is based on Milbank's understanding of the "ontology of peace," or the "absolute priority of peace over violence," which he sees as the "key theme of [Augustine's] entire thought"[38] and then faults him for being inconsistent in allowing the use of religious force.

> Yet Augustine's real mistake here was in the realm of ontology. The revolutionary aspect of his social thought was to deny any ontological purchase to

[35] Hollerich, 321.
[36] Milbank, *Theology and Social Theory*, 432.
[37] Milbank, *Theology and Social Theory*, 407.
[38] Milbank, *Theology and Social Theory*, 390.

> dominium, or power for its own sake.... But his
> account of a legitimate, non-sinful, 'pedagogic'
> coercion violates this ontology, because it makes
> some punishment positive, and ascribes it to the
> action of divine will.... Because punishment must,
> by definition, inflict some harm, however temporary,
> it has an inherently negative, private relationship to
> Being and cannot therefore, by Augustine's own
> lights, escape the taint of sin.[39]

Again, as with Markus, central to Milbank's interpretation of the relationship between heavenly city and earthly peace is his interpretation of 19.17. As with Markus --although with a different reason—he sees a positive connection between the heavenly city and the earthly peace through the Christian ruler,[40] Milbank ultimately finds an inherent problem in "using" earthly peace.

> For the ends sought by the *civitas terrene* are not
> merely limited, finite goods, they are those finite
> goods regarded without "referral" to the infinite
> good, and, in consequence, they are unconditionally
> *bad* ends . . . . For the Church is to make *usus* of the
> peace of this world -- of slavery, "excessive"
> coercion, and compromise between competing
> economic interests. It must never derive these things
> from its own rule and order, and yet should try to
> make them work towards the ultimate purpose, the
> true heavenly peace . . ."[41]

---

[39] Milbank, *Theology and Social Theory*, 420.

[40] While for Markus, the Christian ruler simply functions as an individual Christian, for Milbank, the Christian ruler uses the earthly peace by subordinating it to ecclesiological purpose.

[41] Milbank, *Theology and Social Theory*, 406-407.

Milbank struggles with the data of 19.17, here. On the one hand, he sees that the "ends" of the earthly city (and the earthly peace) are unconditionally "bad ends." On the other hand, the Church is called to use them. Yet at the same time, the use of these bad ends cannot be derived from their own rule. Milbank does not resolve it here, and he does not resolve it in his application of this "use" on the level of the Christian ruler, as a member of the Church:

> Quite clearly, though, there would, for Augustine, be no point in laying down "Christian" norms for an area which was intrinsically sinful. Instead, his nearest approach to political recommendation comes in the form of a "mirror for princes." Here Augustine lays down what qualities will characterize a ruler who also happens to be, as an individual, a member of the Christian Church: he will rule with justice and humility, will be slow to punish and ready to pardon, and so forth. Insofar as is possible, the Christian ruler will make a usus of the earthly peace, by subordinating it to the ecclesial purposes of charity and of a "loving discipline" (the problem here, to which I shall return, is how can such a proper use not simply *negate* the earthly peace altogether?)[42]

Ultimately, for Milbank, there is an inherent problem in "using" earthly peace. In comparing Milbank's understanding of 19.17 with the interpretation at the beginning of the paper, what Milbank seems to be missing is the understanding that, for Augustine, God had ordained the temporal peace and that it is not inherently bad, but that it must be used toward the goal of heavenly peace. For example, Augustine makes it clear that even the "fierceness of war" is included in this temporal peace.[43]

---

[42] Milbank, *Theology and Social Theory*, 407.
[43] Augustine, *City of God* 19.12.

Thus far, we have seen that Markus and Milbank's interpretations of 19.17 are contrasting. Whereas Markus emphasizes the neutrality of the temporal peace, Milbank emphasizes its inherent "badness." Whereas Markus de-emphasizes the heavenly peace on earth ("in its pilgrim state"), Milbank emphasizes it. They both understood Augustine's coercion as essentially a pastoral instrument, and they both saw it as a problem in Augustine's overall understanding of peace, but their interpretations were different. Markus saw it as Augustine's failure to take his "secularization" (desacralization) thesis to its logical conclusion to apply it to church. Milbank saw it as Augustine's betrayal of his "ontology of peace."

Each offers a strength that is a corrective to the other's weakness. Markus's secularization thesis and its realism is an antidote to Milbank's idealistic near-identification of the *City of God* with the visible church. Likewise, Milbank's idealistic ontology-of-peace is an antidote to Markus individualistic and often pessimistic liberal realism with its maximum separation between the visible church and the *City of God*.

What I have shown thus far is that both Markus and Milbank's political theory is strongly tied to their reading of 19.17, and that each of them has read it in a way which tilts the balance which Augustine maintains in the chapter. Milbank tilts the balance on one side (that of using earthly peace), and Markus on the other (that of using it with reference to the heavenly peace).

Jean Bethke Elshtain

Strength of Elshtain's Interpretation

In view of the radical tendencies of Markus and Milbank, others have come forward to find a middle path.[44]   One of the most outspoken among them is Jean Bethke Elshtain.[45]   In *Augustine and the Limit of Politics*, Elshtain develops a political theory primarily based upon Augustine's *City of God*. Especially in the culminating last chapter, Elshtain discusses the views of Robert Markus, John Milbank, and especially Augustine's *City of God* to form her own perspective. Like Markus and Milbank, Elshtain makes the book XIX and especially chapter 17 and its immediate context as the center of her discussion.

She agrees with Markus in repudiating *imperium Christianum*, but she also agrees with Milbank on the "true Christian metanarrative realism" and the priority of peace over war. She accepts Milbank's "code of a peaceful existence" in the *altera civitas* (*City of God* in its pilgrimage), and Markus' critique of peace in the earthly city. Furthermore, like Markus, Elshtain also accepts the legitimacy of the temporal peace, although instead of arguing for the neutrality of the public place, Elshtain argues for the "plurality" of society. It seems clear that Elshtain takes this plurality of society more seriously than either Markus or Milbank. In fact, she is even pluralistic in her methodology; she does a good job of culling from both Markus and Milbank their strengths as well as a host of other people and different fields such as literature, psychology, history, etc. In fact, she is criticized as being liberal by the conservatives, and as being conservative by the liberals.[46]

Weakness of Elshtain's Interpretation

---

[44] Oliver O'Donovan, "Augustine's City of God XIX and Western Political Thought" in Eugene TeSelle, *Living in Two Cities: Augustinian trajectories in political thought* (Scranton: University of Scranton Press, 1998).

[45] Currently the Laura Spelman Rockefeller Professor at the University of Chicago Divinity School.

[46] Max Stackhouse, "Augustine and the Limits of Politics," *Christian Century. A book review.* 114 Ap 23-30 1997, 421.

However, in emphasizing the pluralistic nature of the society, and being pluralistic in her approach, Elshtain's political theory is somewhat incoherent. Yet, a clearly identifiable problem with Elshtain is that there is very little transcendence in the earthly peace. She puts it succinctly: "This peace is attained fitfully in the *altera civitas* in its earthly pilgrimage; *haphazardly, at best, in all earthly cities*; and in its full richness only in the *City of God*, when the time of pressing for the human race in temporality comes to an end."[47] She also says that "peace in its true form as harmony and righteousness is not attainable on this earth, although the hope that keeps alive our longing for it is what stands between us and that emptiness of the abyss."

We can see here a clear departure of Elshtain from Augustine's *City of God* 19.17, in which Augustine described not only the perfect heavenly peace, but also allowed for its possession on this earth, as well as referring the earthly peace to the heavenly peace. Elshtain does not hold to this last point; True peace happens only "haphazardly, at best" in earthly cities. Elshtain misses or circumvents Augustine's emphasis throughout Book XIX on making earthly peace matter by means of referring it to the heavenly peace. In fact, in its place, Elshtain inserts her own moralistic idea. We will see now how this is associated with her interpretation of *City of God* 19.17 and its immediate context.

> On this earth there must be compromises "between human wills" if there is to be anything resembling peace; indeed, the heavenly city on pilgrimage helps to forge peace by calling out "citizens from all nations and so collects a society of aliens, speaking all languages." She -- the *civitas dei* -- does not annul or abolish earthly differences but even "maintains them and follows them," so long as God can be worshipped; in this way, she makes "use of the earthly peace" and it is in her interest, as we

---

[47] Elshtain, *Augustine and a Politics of Limits*, 94. Italics Mine.

might now say, to help to contribute to earthly peace. The life of the saint, like the life of the citizen, is a social life. We are with, and among one another. There must be a balance in our attention to earthly affairs; thus, a person ought not "to be so leisured as to take no thought in that leisure for the interest of his neighbour, nor so active as to feel no need for the contemplation of God." If we are to "promote the well-being of the common people," we must love God and love our neighbor, and the one helps to underscore and animate the other.[48]

There are three departures here from Augustine. Elshtain (1) translates *conpositio uoluntatum* as "compromise between human wills," and not "composition" or agreement. (2) speaks of a "balance" between attending to earthly affair and contemplating God, (3) and says that loving God and loving our neighbor underscore and animate one another.

The idea of "compromise of the wills" smacks of Markus' idea of neutral community, although by itself, we are not certain. More certain are the latter two points, where Elshtain wants to keep the love of God and love of neighbor, as equally valid starting points. This is confirmed in the following page:

> We return, then, to the definition of a commonwealth.... This is where love comes in -- love of God and love of neighbor -- and this is where justice enters as well. Augustine's alternative definition starts with love. "A people is the association of a multitude of rational beings united by a common agreement on the objects of their love." It "follows that to observe the character of a particular people we must examine the objects of its love." No single man can create a commonwealth. There is no

---

[48] Elshtain, *Augustine and a Politics of Limits*, 96.

ur-Founder, no great bringer of order. It begins in ties of fellowship, in households, clans, and tribes, in earthly love and its many discontents.[49]

In contrast, for Augustine, all of Book XIX is predicated on the primacy of the heavenly peace and the need to ground the earthly peace upon it. In fact, the two citations that Elshtain quotes above are taken out of context. The citation about the balance of a life of action and contemplation, cited from19.19, needs to be read in a parallel context of the last sentence: "And yet not even in this case (of pursuing holy leisure) are we obliged wholly to relinquish the sweets of contemplation." The citation about the love of God and neighbor is supposedly cited from 19.20, but the idea is not found there, and the context there is also the same: "if any man uses this life with a *reference* to that other which he ardently loves and confidently hopes for, he may well be called even now blessed...." Thus, although she includes the love of God as a factor, its relationship with the love of neighbor is minimal. The result is that Elshtain's solution to peace becomes moralistic.

This also can be seen in her idea of the earthly peace "participating" in the heavenly peace.

> If the Christian is a disturber of a false peace, he or she yearns for a more authentic representation of earthly peace as that which partakes in the *pax aeterna*. One can hope for what is possible to obtain. An imperfect but nonetheless real earthly peace lies within the realm of the possible.... But our life of fellowship calls us, not to perfection, but to relative peace. The Heavenly City is a perfect vision of peace. But there is earthly work to be done in the name of peace.[50]

---

[49] Elstain, *Augustine and a Politics of Limits*, 97.
[50] Elshtain, *Augustine and a Politics of Limits*, 105.

This idea that earthly peace, by itself, "participates" in the eternal peace is foreign to Augustine. If the earthly peace is directed or motivated by eternal peace, the idea would be entirely that of Augustine. Elshtain never comes around to stating that. In fact as she closes out the chapter as well as the book, she confirms the lack of transcendence in the world and the moral solution to that problem.

> That place, then, which is promised as a dwelling of such peace and security is eternal, and is reserved for eternal beings in "the mother, the Jerusalem which is free". . . [Yet], in this world of discontinuities and profound yearnings, of sometimes terrible necessities, a human being can yet strive to maintain or to create an order that approximates justice . . .[51]

Comparing the Three with Augustine

What I have shown so far is the centrality of the interpretation of the *City of God* 19.17 for each of the three Augustinian political theorists, and how each of them has tilted the balance between maintaining the real possibility of the citizens of the heavenly city promoting earthly peace, and doing so with reference to the heavenly peace, that is with reference to the transcendent reality of God's love in Christ.

In their respective interpretations, each of the three scholars highlighted one aspect above another, inasmuch as each of them had a vested interest in that aspect. For example, the payoff of Markus' interpretation is that of a neutral state in which Christians are free to participate so long as their religious allegiances are not violated. On the one hand, Markus sought to protect Christian's freedom; on the

---

[51] Elshtain, *Augustine and a Politics of Limits*, 110-111.

other, he wanted to create the room for "disturbing the false peace." For Milbank, his interpretation sought to emphasize the importance of the role of the Church in restoring true peace, and in criticizing the inherent evil in any form of physical power. Elshtain sought after a more middle path between Markus and Milbank, trying to maintain some "chastened form of civic virtue"[52] yet at the same time find some transcendent mooring.

Yet, I have shown that each of the scholar's interpretation came with great costs. Markus turned Augustine's *saeculum* from a temporal concept into a neutral space, which invited the notion of a liberal, secular state, which is founded on contract and consent, and which lacks transcendental legitimation. Milbank's interpretation denies the legitimate role of discipline, and has the tendency to see government as being inherently evil. Elshtain's interpretation tries to get the best of both of Markus and Milbank, but ends up losing the distinctive of both. In the end, her perspective is neither distinctly secular, nor distinctly Christian.

Against these renderings, Augustine's own view is much more distinct and robust. His view is distinctly Christian and distinctly secular -- that is, in the sense of encompassing and engaging the *saeculum*. To be sure, Augustine is not a perfectionist, nor can the heavenly peace be experienced in its perfection on earth.[53] Yet, individuals and communities alike *can* experience heavenly peace by the means of faith, and in the context of earthly peace, by first themselves possessing the heavenly peace by faith, and then by referring the earthly peace to the heavenly peace. Augustine calls for a life that is fully social and transcendent. It is truly social because it is truly transcendent.

Conclusion

---

[52] Elshtain, *Augustine and a Politics of Limits*, 91.
[53] Augustine, *City of God,* 529. XIX.27.

We have seen a good example of Augustine's political view in practice in his letter to Darius above. Here we see another one, perhaps even a better one, in one of the letters which Peter Brown mentions among the "new evidences." Brown notes that the words in this letter are "Augustine's last word, to a hitherto unknown interlocutor, on the purpose of his life as a writer."[54] This interlocutor is discovered to be Firmus, a cultivated nobleman of Carthage, whose wife was baptized, but who himself remained uncommitted even after reading the *City of God*. It is to him that Augustine writes,

> So while you may be more learned in doctrine, she is more secure [of her salvation] by reason of her knowledge of the mysteries.... And so, in effect, you are throwing away the fruits of all those books you love. What fruits? Not that some [who read the *City of God*] may have some interesting reading nor that they may learn a number of things they had not known before. But that the readers [of the *City of God*] may be convinced of the [real] "*City of God*" [the reality of that Heavenly Jerusalem that awaited the faithful in the Catholic church]; that they might enter into that "*City of God*" without delay and, once entered, be all the more moved to stay within it, entering it first through re-birth [in baptism] and then continuing through love of righteousness. If those by whom these books are read and praised do not actually take action and do these things, of what good are the books?[55]

The value of this letter is in that it summarizes the core message of the Augustine's magnum opus *The City of God*. Augustine conveys here that the point of the *City of God* is to show

---

[54] Peter Brown, *Augustine of Hippo* (London: Faber and Faber, 2000), 472.
[55] Brown, 471-472.

that the heavenly city (in its pilgrim state) is neither about entering into some narrow religious sect nor being restricted in his social or political influence. On the contrary, by faith ("through re-birth"), one not only enters the city of God and enjoys God (possessing heavenly peace), but "having once entered," will be *truly* motivated to love righteousness, and truly motivated to do the right things -- as in, referring all good actions toward God and man to the attainment of the heavenly peace.

Bibliography

Augustine, *City of God.* Trans. Marcus Dods. [Nicene and Post-Nicene Fathers Series] Chicago: Encyclopaedia Britannica, Inc., 1952.

----. *The City of God.* Trans. R. W. Dyson. Cambridge: Cambridge University Press, 1998.

----. http://ccat.sas.upenn.edu/jod/ These texts were compiled in conjunction with the AugustinusLexikon' project. Würzburg/Gießen, Germany by C. P. Mayer, O.S.A.

----. *The City of God.* Trans. John Healey. Ed. R. V. G. Tasker. New York: E. P. Dutton, 1962.

----. *On Christian Doctrine.* Trans. D. W. Robertson, Jr. Upper Saddle River: Prentice Hall, 1997.

----. *Political Writings.* Trans. Michael W. Tkacz and Douglas Kries. Indianapolis: Hackett Publishing Company, 1994.

----. *Political Writings.* Ed. E. M. Atkins and R. J. Dodaro. Cambridge: Cambridge University Press, 2001.

----. *The City of God.* New York: Fathers of the Church, 1954.

Bowden, Geoffrey C. *The Church Public or Private? An Analysis of the Work of Jean Bethke Elshtain.* A Class Paper at Baylor, 1996.

Brown, Peter. *Augustine of Hippo.* London: Faber and Faber, 2000.

Calvin, John. *Institutes of the Christian Religion.* Ed. John T. McNeill. Philadelphia: The Westminster Press, 1960.

Deane, Herbert A. "Augustine and the State: The Return of Order Upon Disorder." *The City of God: A Collection of Essays.* Ed. Dorothy F. Donnelly. New York: Peter Lang, 1995.

Dekkers, Eligius. *Clavis Patrum Latinorum.* Steenbrugis: In Abbatia Sancti Petri, 1995.

Elshtain, Jean Bethke. *Augustine and a Politics of Limits.* Notre Dame: University of Notre Dame Press, 1995.

----. *Democracy on Trial.* New York: BasicBooks, 1995.

----. *Real Politics: At the Center of Everyday Life.* Baltimore: The Johns Hopkins University Press, 1997.

----. *Religion in American Public Life: Living With Our Deepest Differences.* New York: W. W. Norton & Company, 2001.

----. *Who Are We?: Critical Reflections and Hopeful Possibilities.* Grand Rapids: Eerdmans, 2000.

----. "Why Augustine? Why Now?" *Theology Today* 55 (April 1998), pp. 5-14.

----. *Women and War.* New York: Basic Books, 1987.

Hollerich, Michael J. "Milbank and Augustine" in *History, Apocalypse, and the Secular Imagination: New Essays on Augustine's City of* God. Ed. Mark Vessey, Karla Pollmann, Allen D. Fitzgerald, O.S.A. Bowling Green: Bowling Green State University, 1999.

Markus, R.A. *Saeculum: History and Society in the Theology of St. Augustine.* Cambridge: Cambridge University Press, 1970.

Milbank, John. *Theology & Social Theory: Beyond Secular Reason.* Oxford: Blackwell, 1993.

----. "An Essay Against Secular Order," *Journal of Religious Ethics* 15 no 2 (Fall 1987), pp. 199-224.

O'Daly, Gerald. *Augustine's City of God: A Reader's Guide.* Oxford: Clarenden Press, 1999.

O'Donovan, Oliver. "Augustine's *City of God* XIX and Western Political Thought," in *The City of God: A Collection of Essays.* Ed. Dorothy F. Donnelly. New York: Peter Lang, 1995.

----. "Two Conceptions of Political Authority: Augustine, *De Civitate Dei*, XIX. 14-15, and Some Thirteenth-Century Interpretations," *The City of God: A Collection of Essays.* Ed. Dorothy F. Donnelly. New York: Peter Lang, 1995.

Stackhouse, Max. "Augustine and the Limits of Politics," *Christian Century* 114 (April 23-30, 1997), pp. 421-424.

Teselle, Eugene. *Living in Two Cities: Augustinian Trajectories in Political Thought.* Scranton: University of Scranton Press, 1998.

----. "Toward an Augustinian Politics," *Journal of Religious Ethics* 16 (Spring, 1988), pp. 87-108.

"And when you hear that we look for a kingdom, you suppose, without making any inquiry, that we speak of a human kingdom; whereas we speak of that which is with God, as appears also from the confession of their faith made by those who are charged with being Christians, though they know that death is the punishment awarded to him who so confesses. For if we looked for a human kingdom, we should also deny our Christ, that we might not be slain; and we should strive to escape detection, that we might obtain what we expect. But since our thoughts are not fixed on the present, we are not concerned when men cut us off; since also death is a debt which must at all events be paid."

Justin Martyr

The First Apology

Death Penalty and Jesus Christ: Some Initial Thoughts

Christian Kim
University of Cambridge
UK

Does Jesus oppose the Death Penalty? This is a question not often addressed directly even by theologians. In this short essay, I will make a preliminary study of the question. Hopefully, this will spur further discussion, and I hope to have the opportunity to write a more in-depth study on the subject in the near future.

The answer to the question regarding Jesus Christ's support of Capital Punishment is a resounding "Yes" from the vantage point of the New Testament. Here, I will forward three points as supporting my claim. They are: (1) Jesus Christ's support of governmental authority with implicit support of its right to carry out the Death Penalty; (2) Jesus Christ's acceptance of unjust Death Penalty carried out against John the Baptist; (3) Jesus Christ's acceptance of the Death Penalty carried out against Him despite the clear tainting of the legal process. Now, I will treat each of these cases more closely.

Firstly, Jesus explicitly supports government authority as a matter of principle. The best example of Jesus Christ's support of government authority can be found in Mark 12:13-17. The enemies of Jesus Christ try to trick Jesus into saying incriminating things against himself in order to arrest him. The question addressed to Jesus is: Is it right to pay taxes to Caesar or not? The expectation that Jewish leaders have in asking this question is that Jesus would say, "No."

The expectation is clearly evident in the way the question is prefaced in verse 14: "Teacher, we know you are a man of integrity. You aren't swayed by men, because you pay no attention to who they are; but you teach the way of God in accordance with the truth." The Jewish leaders are basically challenging Jesus' bravery. They are essentially saying: "You say you are a representative of God and you don't fear men. So, tell us, should we be opposed to paying taxes to the government that has no respect for God?"

Given that Jesus is preaching the message of the Kingdom of God, the Pharisees and the Herodians could reasonably expect a "No" answer from Jesus. Since His followers are members of the Kingdom of God, they should be loyal to that Kingdom and not to the kingdom on earth. They should not pay taxes to a government that opposes worship of God. So, in principle the followers of Jesus should pay taxes to the Kingdom of God and its representatives and not to the earthly kingdom that does not support the worship of God. Is not paying taxes to Caesar an evidence of weakness and opposition to the Kingdom of God principle?

However, contrary to the logical expectation of Jesus Christ's Kingdom of God message, Jesus sets out the Christian principle on taxation. It is Jesus' principle that taxes be paid to Caesar. Jesus replies in Mark 12:17: "Give to Caesar what is Caesar's and to God what is God's." Jesus states as a civil law of the Christian faith that they pay taxes to the secular government, even if it is hostile to God. The Catholic Church and other Christian denominations have fundamentally upheld this principle on taxation. The Catholic Church will not tell a Catholic in Sadam Hussein's government not to pay taxes. Protestant denominations will not tell a North Korean to withhold paying taxes to the Communist government. This is because Jesus Christ clearly states Christian civil regulation regarding taxation.

Why is this important as a principle? In the Old Testament, Israel has a type of theocracy with the implicit understanding that the government is under the authority of God. Thus, taxes levied should be paid because it is a government instituted by God. The problem rises when Israel comes under secular rule that is opposed to the worship of God. Jesus is asked to state a principle that is highly debated. Many Jews pay taxes to Caesar because they have to and not because they think it is the right thing to do. How is it right to pay taxes to an unjust government which opposes God? The question can be addressed more radically. Should Catholics in Nazi Germany pay taxes to Hitler's government? In light of Jesus Christ's principle for the Christian faith, the answer is "Yes." Not paying taxes to Hitler's government or Caesar's government which oppresses the worship of God would go against civil laws of the Kingdom of God.

Jesus resolves the question of taxation by an unjust, oppressive government once and for all for the Christian faith. Fundamentally, Jesus supports the right of the secular government to carry out its governmental functions to the same extent that the theocracy of the Old Testament is allowed to carry out its governmental practices. This principle of Jesus is revolutionary for the first century AD in Palestine.

Furthermore, there is the implicit assumption in Jesus' teaching that a secular (even hostile to God) government has the right to carry out other rights that the theocracy has in the Old Testament. For instance, Jesus never questions the right of governments to wage wars. The question of a righteous war is a non-issue. The fact that Jesus lives at a time when the government of Caesar acquires rule over Palestine by war and that this government is a military expansionist government is significant. As a Christian principle, Jesus does not oppose military expansion nor wars. Jesus never decries the innocent lives lost in unjust wars. Jesus fundamentally assumes that governments, whether a theocracy or Caesar's, have the right to carry out wars and kill people in the process.

The principle that a secular government has the right to carry out punishments is also implicitly accepted. As Israel's theocracy is expected to carry out punishments for crimes, Caesar's government is as well. Jesus does not challenge the Death Penalty, either implicitly or explicitly. Capital Punishment is an important part of Israel's government practice in the Old Testament, and it is divinely favored (and mandated!) punishment in Biblical Law.

Jesus Christ does not condemn Old Testament sanction of government carrying out the Death Penalty. More importantly, Jesus does not condemn a secular government's right to carry out the Death Penalty.

At the time of Jesus, there is the highly visible way of carrying out the Death Penalty. People are hung up on crosses by civil government authorities. Jesus never condemns their right to carry out the Death Sentences against criminals. This point is very important in light of the fact that many worshippers of God are *unjustly* put to the Death Sentence. For instance, a religious worshipper of God may revolt when the Roman authorities try to defile the Temple. These people could be put to death for trying to uphold their religious worship. Jesus does not condemn the civil government for putting religious people to death. There is the implicit understanding that even if those who are righteous in the eyes of God are put to death unjustly by the civil government, it is acceptable in the eyes of God.

As a matter of principle, Jesus Christ fundamentally supports the government's right to put people to death. Even governments that are hostile to God and worship of God have the fundamental right to carry out the Death Sentence. Even if people of faith are killed for their faith by governments hostile to the faith, Jesus accepts the governmental right to carry out the Death Sentence. The fact that the innocent may be killed unknowingly or knowingly by a government is *not* an issue for Jesus Christ in putting forth the Christian position on government duties and rights.

Perhaps, this point is most clearly illustrated in the second case. Jesus accepts the unjust Death Sentence carried out against John the Baptist in Matthew 14:1-14. Before discussing this passage, it is important to recognize that different governments have different structures for carrying out justice. When ancient Israel is a theocracy, there is a system of stoning criminals to death. But when Jews are not in control of Israel, they are not allowed to practice this form of execution, which is not condoned by the current government in power.

It is clear that Jesus condemns Jewish individuals usurping Roman right to execution. In John 8:1ff., Jesus tells people not to stone a woman caught in adultery to death as required according to the Law of Moses because they do not have the legitimate (secular) authority to do so. They are under Roman civil and criminal laws and not under ancient Israel's. While condemning the ancient Jewish system current under Old Testament theocracy, Jesus never opposes Roman government's right to carry out the Death Penalty according to its system of laws. Romans do not execute for adultery while Jews want to. Jesus, by stopping the stoning of the adulterous woman, is upholding the rule of law by civil magistrates.

In this light, Jesus supports every government's right, regardless of its character, to carry out the Death Penalty according to its own legal system. Jesus does not challenge whether a government is righteous or not. In fact, there is perhaps no government so opposed to divine worship as the Roman government. In this light, the Nazis have the right to carry out the Death Penalty according to their laws. Sadam Hussein has the right to carry out the Death Penalty by his laws. Jesus never defends the exclusive right of a certain government (for instance, the Old Testament theocracy) to carry out the Death Penalty. All governments are legitimate, regardless of their character, and they have the fundamental right to carry out the Death Penalty according to their system of laws (however against the worship of God).

Jesus Christ's recognition of fundamental rights of the secular government is revolutionary. In the case of John the Baptist, it seems unfair to our modern sensibilities. John the Baptist is arrested by Herod, the civil magistrate, because John speaks against him for marrying his brother Philip's wife. In his world, Herod has the right – the legal right – to arrest John in this manner to the same extent that Caesar has the right to arrest those who commit treason against him. Although legally acceptable by the standards of that government, one might say it is unfair.

Jesus Christ never challenges the right of a secular government – however unjust or opposed to God – to round up those under their authority, even for unfair reasons. Nowhere in the Bible will anyone find Jesus' condemnation of Herod's arrest of John the Baptist. In fact, the Gospel account clearly indicates that Jesus has no objection to the Death Sentence carried out against John the Baptist.

This point is very important because of the unfair nature of the Death Sentence. John the Baptist is arrested for "speaking against the crown." His death sentence is imposed as the result of a whim of the supreme ruler of his region. He has the legal right to kill John the Baptist, as a king does in a monarchy.

Jesus never criticizes Herod's carrying out of the Death Penalty in the confines of his legitimacy as defined in that government. This is an important point to emphasize. For Jesus, it does not matter whether a government is righteous or not. What Jesus cares about is that a legitimate government (that which is in place) has the right to carry out its governmental duties and rights as self-defined by that government.

Perhaps, Jesus' attitude towards the unjust Death Penalty of John the Baptist best outlines the Christian attitude towards the Death Penalty. Death Penalty can be carried out by any government – whether righteous or unrighteous, for God or against God -- in the way it sees fit.

This point is best illustrated in the third case. Jesus is crucified by the Jews via the agency of Roman authorities. The Gospels clearly show Jews conniving to kill Jesus. Jews try to stone Jesus Christ and kill Him through the Jewish Death Sentence method found in the Old Testament (John 10:31). Jesus does not allow this to happen. Jesus fundamentally opposes Jewish usurpation of civil authority belonging to Roman-appointed agents. Jesus' preferred mode of death is through the legally sanctioned means of the cross (however unfair or contaminated the system).

The Gospels detail clearly and at length to the contamination of the legal process. Jewish leaders try to trap Jesus Christ and trick him to say seditious, terrorist, and treasonous statements in order to arrest him (Luke 20:20). This is a type of entrapment. Most of things said in "leading the witness" is not admissible in court as a case against him. But ancient Palestine is different.

Jewish authorities fail at getting terrorist and seditious words from Jesus, so they try to frame him by producing false witnesses (Matthew 26:59-60; Luke 23:1-2). The Gospel accounts are emphatic in showing that Jewish leaders collude to produce false accusers and fictitious testimonies. Jewish leaders are clearly guilty of conspiracy. Jewish authorities further attempt to taint the legal system by producing a false charge against Jesus for sedition ("King of the Jews") so that the legitimate Roman authority would kill Jesus Christ for treason. Jewish leaders actively lobbying unwilling civil magistrates to kill Jesus is described in no uncertain terms in the New Testament (Luke 23:4-5, 10, 13-17).

Not only do Jewish leaders attempt to lobby at the top for unfair execution of Jesus Christ, Jewish leaders instigate the masses to near riot to compel the unwilling civil magistrates to order the Death Penalty. Details of instigating violence are clearly outlined in the Gospels (Matthew 27:19-26).

The Gospels clearly portray Jewish leaders as manipulating and corrupting legal process in whichever possible way to get the Death Sentence for Jesus. If anyone suffers an unfair Death Penalty – one most tainted – it is Jesus Christ.

However, nowhere in the Gospel accounts does Jesus Christ object to the institution of the death penalty. Fundamental support of the death penalty is presented in the New Testament. Nowhere else in the New Testament, even years after the infliction of the unjust Death Penalty on Jesus, do New Testament writers condemn the Death Penalty. They all know that the innocent died. Details of corrupting right legal process are elaborated on *ad nauseam*. In light of this, the New Testament clearly supports Jesus' position on the Death Penalty as legitimate. It is in line with God's law to grant secular powers – however unrighteous or opposed to God – the right to sentence those in their realm to death. Even if there is tainting of legal process or instigation of the masses to influence legal ruling, the right to carry out Death Sentence by the government that is in place (whether monarchy, democracy, or whichever other form) is fundamentally upheld by Jesus' faith-system.

The only objection Jesus makes during His trial is against the obstruction of justice (delivered by those who represent the government). When a guard tries to arrest Jesus, one of his disciples takes out his sword to kill the guard. He succeeds only in striking the ear off of the guard. Jesus heals the ear of the guard and rebukes his disciple. Jesus is recognizing the guard's duty. Jesus fundamentally recognizes the right of a secular government – even those opposed to God and righteousness – to arrest and carry out the Death Penalty, even unrighteously.

Jesus Christ fundamentally acknowledges that the secular government (even the most unethical and that which is opposed to God) has the right to carry out its governmental rights in the same way that the theocracy of the Old Testament has. This includes the carrying out of the Death Penalty. Jesus allows the government to self-define its process of carrying out the Capital Punishment. Jesus never even hints at destroying the Death Penalty. As a principle, just like taxation, the government has the fundamental right under God's law to carry out the Death Penalty, even in cases they are fundamentally in error about a person's innocence (either consciously or unintentionally).

Also, from The Hermit Kingdom Press....

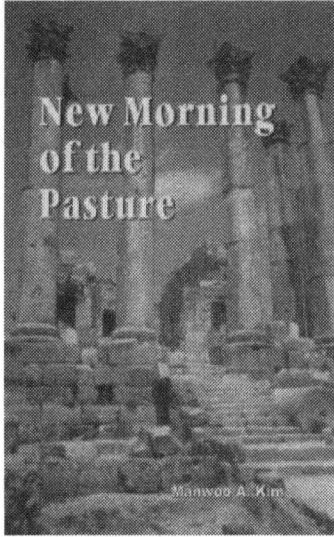

Rev. Manwoo A. Kim's Devotional Poems

New Morning of the Pasture:
Poetic Reflections of a Korean American Pastor

ISBN 0-97238-641-6

Published in 2003 (pp. 117, paperback 6 x 9)
Price: US$12.99 (£9.99 & €13.99)

*Included Essay: "The Korean Diaspora's Realized Vision"

http://www.TheHermitKingdomPress.com